T0128200

DIRT BAGS, LIARS AND POWER FREAKS

A critical look at the IRS, DOJ and politicians

Douglas P. Rosile Sr.

authorHOUSE®

AuthorHouse™
1663 Liberty Drive
Bloomington, IN 47403
www.authorhouse.com
Phone: 1 (800) 839-8640

Published by AuthorHouse 01/18/2017

ISBN: 978-1-5246-5847-2 (sc)
ISBN: 978-1-5246-5846-5 (e)

Library of Congress Control Number: 2017900242

CONTENTS

PROLOGUE/INTRODUCTION

Former Supreme Court Justice Oliver Wendall Holmes Jr., (1902-1932) once said "Taxes are what we pay for a civilized society". That quote is inscribed on the IRS headquarters in Washington, D.C.

I want to pose this question: are we now a "civilized" society? And then ask what "civilized" society would have such an unintelligible, corrupt, abusive income tax system run by trained terrorists.

While Justice Holmes comment implies the government needs money to operate and others would agree by quoting the Scripture about "rendering unto Caesar…" I would question, how much the federal government truly NEEDS to effectively operate and whether the government ought to collect it under threat, duress, coercion, intimidation and fear of bodily harm. Ultimately, the issue centers on this question: how much of your money should you be able to keep?

Everything we have comes from God, belongs to God, and yet he only wants ten percent for his kingdom, and that number hasn't changed over thousands of years. The Scriptures also teach that we should all share our good fortune with the poor. "From everyone who has been given much, much will be demanded; and from the one who has been entrusted with much, much more will be asked. To those that have been given much, much is expected" (Luke 12:48). He doesn't say to pass it through the hands of bureaucratic dirtbags, liars and power freaks first.

After reading extensively about government waste, fraud and corruption I think the obvious answer to the second question is a whole lot less than they are now stealing[1]. Unfortunately you can bet the talking heads, bureaucrats and politicians will never tell you the truth even if they knew it. I discuss this in detail in the third part of this book.

During the entire budget mess after the 2010 midterm election, and again in 2012, 2014 and the 2016 presidential election candidates failed to discuss the issues of waste, fraud and corruption. The message constantly given by Democrats and the Obama administration focused on taxing the rich. Every time a contrived "fiscal cliff" looms leaders still refuse to address waste, fraud and corruption. Some have suggested we can't cut our way to fiscal sanity. However the truth is that real budget restraint means fewer giveaways, fewer moochers, fewer overpriced weapons of mass destruction and more unemployed bureaucrats, most of which is a loss for progressives/liberals, but a win for hard working Americans.

An old joke used to be, the three largest terrorist organizations in the world were the PLO, the IRA and the IRS, not necessarily in that order. While Al-Qaeda and ISIS may have replaced the Irish Republican Army and the PLO in the news, the point is still the same. The IRS is not the customer-friendly agency they would have Americans believe. If one defines terrorism as the attempt to induce a desired behavior by the abuse of authority or the use of duress, coercion and intimidation then the IRS falls within this definition and operates as the single largest domestic terrorist organization in the United States today.

The sad truth remains they are not a legally authorized agency of the United States of America and continue to survive with the protection of a totally corrupt legal system and cowardly politicians. This book will educate America as to why the IRS exists, and more importantly why citizens/voters must abolish the present tax system. This book will also

---

[1]   Grace Commission report Jan. 1984; Martin Gross, two books, *The Government Racket-Washington Waste from A to Z*, 1992 and 2000 Harper Collins Publishing; Ross Perot, 1992 *United We Stand How We Take Back America*

address the corrupt legal system and fainthearted politicians who give the IRS support, written from the perspective of my own experiences as a former professional accountant for 35 years, a co-defendant in the Wesley Snipes case and a guest of the government for three and a half years.

The Founding Fathers never envisioned a government that would steal the fruits of the people's labor. The "Robin Hood" mentality of redistributing wealth has done nothing but chase capital and jobs out of America (which Mr. Trump wants to bring back) and given rise to a whole generation of people brainwashed to believe they are "entitled" to free benefits. They commit their vote to the liberal politicians in exchange for the promise of these perceived "entitlements".

Those who identify with either the Democrats or Republicans may not want to continue reading this book since both parties contribute to the problem not the solution. No other party has controlled Congress or the White House since 1877. This books speaks to those who register as Independent, Libertarian, a member of the Reform Party, Green Party, Constitution Party or the Rent is to Damn High Party and have the courage to act upon their convictions. Additionally, this book addresses those who constitute 61% of the population under 45 years old who desire a better future for themselves and their families, not as a financial slave whom the government spies upon and controls. It is time to help wake up America.

RE-ELECT NOBODY is the starting point.

Part One
THE INCOME TAX

CHAPTER ONE

WHY THE SYSTEM EXITS

The personal income tax has been around just over 100 plus years and was the creation of the Wilson Administration, one of the most corrupt in our history.[2] It originally required only a three page form, with the tax only 1% of taxable income under $20,000 (that's about $480,000 in 2015 dollars). The highest rate was 7%. A copy of that return is below. That return did not require a "slave surveillance number" (SSN) or signature under penalty of perjury. Originally, the income tax did not affect every citizen nor did the law consist of more pages than the Bible. However as soon as the politicians began to "tinker with the tax code" this changed.

The war against "taxation without representation" has taken a turn for the worse. Representation has soured. A tax cheat, Tim Geithner, was running the Treasury Department and another, Charlie Rangel, formerly the House Ways and Means Committee. Both had forgotten to report part of their income. Worse, most of the money stolen from Americans is wasted on vote buying socialist programs, countless "pork barrel" projects, a government pension for people who created the mess and wasted the money, and building overpriced weapons of mass destruction in the name of national security.

---

[2] The National Interest website, 11/5/14, Robert Merry

Form 1040.

INCOME TAX.

THE PENALTY
FOR FAILURE TO HAVE THIS RETURN IN
THE HANDS OF THE COLLECTOR OF
INTERNAL REVENUE ON OR BEFORE
MARCH 1 IS $20 TO $1,000.
(SEE INSTRUCTIONS ON PAGE 4.)

UNITED STATES INTERNAL REVENUE.

RETURN OF ANNUAL NET INCOME OF INDIVIDUALS.

(As provided by Act of Congress, approved October 3, 1913.)

RETURN OF NET INCOME RECEIVED OR ACCRUED DURING THE YEAR ENDED DECEMBER 31, 191 ....

(FOR THE YEAR 1913, FROM MARCH 1, TO DECEMBER 31.)

Filed by (or for) .... of ....
(Full name of individual.)   (Street and No.)

in the City, Town, or Post Office of .... State of ....

(Fill in pages 2 and 3 before making entries below.)

1. GROSS INCOME (see page 2, line 12)	$
2. GENERAL DEDUCTIONS (see page 3, line 7)	$
3. NET INCOME	$

Deductions and exemptions allowed in computing income subject to the normal tax of 1 per cent.

4. Dividends and net earnings received or accrued, of corporations, etc., subject to like tax. (See page 2, line 11)	$
5. Amount of income on which the normal tax has been deducted and withheld at the source. (See page 2, line 9, column A)	
6. Specific exemption of $3,000 or $4,000, as the case may be. (See Instructions 3 and 19)	

Total deductions and exemptions. (Items 4, 5, and 6) . . . . $

7. TAXABLE INCOME on which the normal tax of 1 per cent is to be calculated. (See Instruction 3) . $

8. When the net income shown above on line 3 exceeds $20,000, the additional tax thereon must be calculated as per schedule below:

						INCOME.	TAX.
1	per cent on amount over $20,000 and not exceeding $50,000 . .					$	$
2	"	"	50,000	"	"	75,000 .		
3	"	"	75,000	"	"	100,000 .		
4	"	"	100,000	"	"	250,000 .		
5	"	"	250,000	"	"	500,000 .		
6	"	"	500,000	. . . .				

Total additional or super tax . . . . $

Total normal tax (1 per cent of amount entered on line 7) . . $

Total tax liability . . . . $

GROSS INCOME.

This statement must show in the proper spaces the entire amount of gains, profits, and income received by or accrued to the individual from all sources during the year specified on page 1.

DESCRIPTION OF INCOME.	A. Amount of income on which tax has been deducted and withheld at the source.	B. Amount of income on which tax has NOT been deducted and withheld at the source.
1. Total amount derived from salaries, wages, or compensation for personal service of whatever kind and in whatever form paid	$	$
2. Total amount derived from professions, vocations, businesses, trade, commerce, or sales or dealings in property, whether real or personal, growing out of the ownership or use of interest in real or personal property, including bonds, stocks, etc.		
3. Total amount derived from rents and from interest on notes, mortgages, and securities (other than reported on lines 5 and 6)		
4. Total amount of gains and profits derived from partnership business, whether the same be divided and distributed or not		
5. Total amount of fixed and determinable annual gains, profits, and income derived from interest upon bonds and mortgages or deeds of trust, or other similar obligations of corporations, joint-stock companies or associations, and insurance companies, whether payable annually or at shorter or longer periods		
6. Total amount of income derived from coupons, checks, or bills of exchange for or in payment of interest upon bonds issued in *foreign countries* and upon *foreign mortgages* or like obligations (not payable in the United States), and also from coupons, checks, or bills of exchange for or in payment of any dividends upon the stock or interest upon the obligations of foreign corporations, associations, and insurance companies engaged in business in foreign countries		
7. Total amount of income received from fiduciaries		
8. Total amount of income derived from any source whatever, not specified or entered elsewhere on this page		
9. TOTALS		
NOTES.—Enter total of Column A on line 5 of first page.		
10. AGGREGATE TOTALS OF COLUMNS A AND B	$	
11. Total amount of income derived from dividends on the stock or from the net earnings of corporations, joint-stock companies, associations, or insurance companies subject to like tax (To be entered on line 4 of first page.)	$	
12. TOTAL "Gross Income" (to be entered on line 1 of first page)	$	

3

GENERAL DEDUCTIONS.

1. The amount of necessary expenses actually paid in carrying on business, but not including business expenses of partnerships, and not including personal, living, or family expenses .	$			
2. All interest paid within the year on personal indebtedness of taxpayer				
3. All national, State, county, school, and municipal taxes paid within the year (not including those assessed against local benefits)				
4. Losses actually sustained during the year incurred in trade or arising from fires, storms, or shipwreck, and not compensated for by insurance or otherwise				
5. Debts due which have been actually ascertained to be worthless and which have been charged off within the year				
6. Amount representing a reasonable allowance for the exhaustion, wear, and tear of property arising out of its use or employment in the business, not to exceed, in the case of mines, 5 per cent of the gross value at the mine of the output for the year for which the computation is made, but no deduction shall be made for any amount of expense of restoring property or making good the exhaustion thereof, for which an allowance is or has been made . . .				
7. Total "GENERAL DEDUCTIONS" (to be entered on line 2 of first page)				

AFFIDAVIT TO BE EXECUTED BY INDIVIDUAL MAKING HIS OWN RETURN.

I solemnly swear (or affirm) that the foregoing return, to the best of my knowledge and belief, contains a true and complete statement of all gains, profits, and income received by or accrued to me during the year for which the return is made, and that I am entitled to all the deductions and exemptions entered or claimed therein, under the Federal Income-tax Law of October 3, 1913.

Sworn to and subscribed before me this ....

day of ...., 191   ....
                                                            (Signature of individual.)

SEAL OF OFFICER TAKING AFFIDAVIT.	....
	....
	(Official capacity.)

AFFIDAVIT TO BE EXECUTED BY DULY AUTHORIZED AGENT MAKING RETURN FOR INDIVIDUAL.

I solemnly swear (or affirm) that I have sufficient knowledge of the affairs and property of ....
to enable me to make a full and complete return thereof, and that the foregoing return, to the best of my knowledge and belief, contains a true and complete statement of all gains, profits, and income received by or accrued to said individual during the year for which the return is made, and that the said individual is entitled, under the Federal Income-tax Law of October 3, 1913, to all the deductions and exemptions entered or claimed therein.

Sworn to and subscribed before me this ....

day of ...., 191   ....
                                                            (Signature of agent.)

ADDRESS IN FULL ....

SEAL OF OFFICER TAKING AFFIDAVIT.	....
	....
	(Official capacity.)

[SEE INSTRUCTIONS ON BACK OF THIS PAGE.]

I spent 35 years as a professional accountant dealing primarily with middle class Americans and I have an intimate knowledge of why the existing system ought to be abolished.

George Will, a conservative columnist and talking head, once wrote, "The perennial mischief in Washington is using the tax code NOT simply to raise revenue efficiently (with minimal distortion of economic behavior) but to pamper pet causes, appease muscular interests and make social policy. Since 1986 the tax code has acquired more than 15,000 complications". (Washington Post, Dec. 2010.)

That quote suggests the four reasons the present day tax system primarily exists:

a) To shakedown organizations and people for campaign donations and as a weapon to be used against the political enemies of the party in power. "The tax code has become complicated because Congress uses it to reward or punish companies or causes, which it favors or opposes."[3] It's the "You want legislation, I want a donation" mentality, or the "If you don't donate I'll sponsor a bill to penalize your industry". (Do you think Obamacare is penalizing the medical profession?) Denying tax exempt status to suppress the free speech rights of entities trying to organize that have a different political viewpoint is also a common practice as Tea Party organizations can attest to.

Realistically everybody belongs to some "special interest group". You may be a senior citizen, a trial lawyer, a gun owner, a doctor, a teacher, a union member, an accountant, a tree hugger, a retiree, a minority, gay or a veteran. Many of us identify with more than one group. Each of these groups unleashes its dogs (lobbyists) on Congressmen/Congresswomen and Senators to get some break, handout or legislation for you. Your "Congress-critters" in turn expect large scale donations. It now costs about two million dollars to buy a Congressional seat and eight to ten

---

[3]   Cal Thomas, Dec, 2010, Warren, Tribune, *There are language problems*

million to buy a Senate seat. Both of those jobs pay less than $180,000 per year, but come with substantial benefits and power. Yet after making us financial slaves and destroying our freedoms they expect a pension and health care for life. If we had real campaign and election reform (i.e. term limits and spending limits) this would no longer be a problem and one less reason to keep the income tax.

One of the stories in the news that gave credibility to this was the Obama administration's using the IRS to attack the Tea Party movement (and other perceived opponents) regarding the tax exempt status for its various chapters. Wayne Allan Root, [4]who was the Libertarian Party candidate for VP in 2008, made known his attacks by the IRS because he's an active member of Obama's enemies list. You can add Bill O'Reilly, Paula Jones, Glenn Beck's 9/12 Project and me to the list of people attacked by the IRS over the years.

Whether or not one agrees with these individuals' ideas, no civilized society should use its tax system or any other kind of weapon to stifle free speech, especially when the mouths of politicians so freely and loudly proclaim "false speech". Remember, when their lips are moving there's a good chance they're lying! I give you the 2016 Presidential candidates.

In May, 2013 the IRS has issued a lame apology for targeting conservative, Tea Party organizations and Lois Lerner, the IRS official in charge pleaded the 5th when called before Congress. She has since retired, and the attorney general refused to hold her accountable for contempt of Congress.[5]

b) The second reason for the existence of the income tax is to accomplish "social engineering", a fancy term to describe getting people to act or behave in a way that politicians think is best for them and that will allegedly stimulate the economy.

---

[4]   The Blzae, Oct. 8, 2012

[5]   Yahoo News, May, 201 4

They may want you to a) buy a certain kind of car, b) adopt a child, c) save energy, d) get a college education, e) take care of your own retirement, f) get a job, g) buy a distressed home, h) start a business, i) donate to charity, j) develop new technologies, or k) hire certain types of people. The list goes on and on. Congress "tinkers" so much with the tax code that you need a computer or a professional to prepare your tax return, a far cry from the three page, <u>flat tax</u> started in 1913 that was promoted as never going to exceed 7% and would only affect the rich people living in the Northeastern part of the country, since at that time the majority of the population was east of the Mississippi and north of Atlanta. Creating more work for lawyers and tax preparers is also part of social engineering. Many of the tax laws passed in the last three decades should have been subtitled "Welfare and Retirement Act for Lawyers and Accountants". This tinkering of the tax code brings truth to the old adage, "when you know all the answers they change all the questions". The ensuing complexity dissuades taxpayers from doing their own taxes and understanding "the Code.

Encouraging people to do something they would probably do anyway, because it was necessary, intelligent, saved them money or filled a need in their life does not justify a tax system full of deductions, credits and write-offs simply to buy votes and crow about how it allegedly helped the economy. One of the Democratic attack ads in 2012 discussed how Mitt Romney (single-handedly) was going to cut out the mortgage interest deduction, the child care deduction and the educational credits, all of which are good ideas as I will discuss later. Democrats however, want voters to view these as "sacred cows" areas that should remain untouched. I've picked out some of the most common examples of social engineering and will elaborate on the fallacy of each in the next chapter.

c) The third reason the current system exists is to stifle the first amendment rights (free speech) of what are called Section 501(c) 3 organizations, or "tax-exempt organizations". If a minister, priest, rabbi, pastor, imam or other religious leader were to talk negatively about the waste, fraud, corruption, neglect of the poor and abuse that permeates our government or suggest their congregations support a pro-life or traditional marriage candidate they would be attacked by the IRS and threatened with the loss of that special "tax-exempt" status.

I find it appalling that a religious organization or lawfully organized "not-for-profit entity" has to apply to any government entity and be "blessed" by the IRS to operate in this country. The Founding Fathers designed the First Amendment to keep the government out of the churches, NOT the churches out of the government. Where else would these people get their moral compass? Do questionable religious or charitable organizations, churches or cults exist? Sure. But stifling the free speech of all other congregations because of these rogue organizations is not the effective way to deal with them. When much of our country's politics offer a voting choice between bad and worse why shouldn't religious leaders be allowed to criticize or challenge dope smoking, draft dodging, womanizers and other miscreants who want to run (ruin) this country? Aren't we "one nation UNDER GOD"? Clearly this nation has forgotten "under God" as politicians are even afraid to allow the Ten Commandments to be displayed.

I believe church leaders should use the pulpit to preach about the Word of God as it relates to the moral decay of societies. Neither persuasive campaign speeches nor money solve the issue of abortion, drugs, abuse of authority, child molestation, bigotry, wars, violence, racial tensions, "Hollywood marriages", fatherless homes and corrupt governments.

Another facet of this troubling problem resides in the inability to make a "tax deductible" donation to an organization unless the IRS has approved and registered the organization. Heads of charitable organizations sometimes complain that Christian people wouldn't donate if their donations weren't tax deductible. Pure nonsense. People donated and helped others long before we had an income tax. Those who believe in God know it's the right thing to do and pleases Him regardless of the tax deduction. Scripture says the poor will always be with you. (Matthew

26:11) If the politicians let people keep more of THEIR money they would have the ability to donate more to whatever church, charity, person or cause they desire. As a result donations increase and problems would be addressed. Money should not filter through the bureaucracy before it gets to those who need it most.

d) Fourth, the continuation of the income tax allows the government to spy on everyone's financial activities. However, with the passage of the "Turn America into a Police State Act" (aka The Patriot Act), Foreign Intelligence Surveillance Act and FinCen they really don't need the income tax code for that any more. The government prosecutes "organized" crime through financial spying and they like to remind Americans that income tax evasion is how they "got" Al Capone, a famous gangster from the 1920's & 30's. Today with unlimited surveillance by the NSA, warrantless searches, the "Patriot" Act and many other unconstitutional tactics, the federal government no longer has to depend on tax crimes to catch anyone.

These new laws now imply that everybody is a terrorist. After the tragedy of "911" law enforcement had to rethink national security from scratch. Because they now view all Americans as potential terrorists they adopted a "one size fits all" agenda. The federal government now monitors all financial transactions, bank employees' act as undercover cops and any financial transactions, foreign accounts or business structures they don't like are "suspicious activity". As a professional accountant I found that you could tell a lot about a person by simply reviewing their checkbook or spending habits. Ever notice when the cops are investigating somebody the FIRST thing they do is subpoena the "financial records"? They may not find anything criminal, but a "routine" investigation or audit can expose a person's whole life. Information gathered in that process is then "stored" (and shared) for later use. Those of us who adhere to the libertarian idea of "zero government" find the government knowing where I shop, what/where I eat, where I vacation, what books I read, what kind of car I drive, my medical history, the house I own, if I own a gun, who I donate to and ad infinitum, highly troubling, and certainly an obvious invasion of privacy. The government markets this invasion of privacy as the best way to keep us safe from international terrorists. The problem, however centers on who's keeping us safe from the *domestic* terrorists? The shootings at Fort Hood and in Washington DC on military property suggest they can't even protect their own turf.

Every day that the IRS continues to exist, every member of Congress is guilty of aiding and abetting the existence of a domestic terrorist organization while misleading the American public to focus their attention on waging war on terrorism abroad. We have plenty of domestic terrorists, many of them collecting a government paycheck.

No civilized society should tolerate these shabby reasons to justify their income tax system. A humorous but sad quip describes the situation well: "The income tax system has made more liars out of people than the game of golf".

Many of you will scoff and still say, "…but the government needs money too". To this I would respond by asking what constitutes "need?" The true role of government and associated costs to operate it should be simply to safeguard our Constitutional rights, not support politicians, the politicians' pet projects and personal interests. The inability to distinguish the difference between a person's need and his or her wants illustrates how the government currently operates. A person may need transportation, buying a brand new $80,000 "luxury" vehicle fills the need but also serves a want. To be frugal, the person could buy a much more affordable used subcompact because it can move a person from point A to point B, both vehicles have four wheels, tires, seats, brakes and steering. Both have access to the same roads, but only one option fills the need without wasting money on a want. Most Americans do not truly understand what the federal government genuinely "needs". Instead the tendency is to say "we have a problem (that we created) and the only way to solve it is by throwing money at it."

FACT: <u>Presidents don't raise or lower your taxes,</u> they make suggestions, recommendations and propose budgets but Congress must pass a bill in order to raise or lower taxes. The President can veto it, sign it or let it become law without a signature. The president may get the praise or the blame but Congress is the real hero or culprit. When "Congress-critters" worry more about their own re-election and sacrifice progress and change for power the people always lose.

In January, 2012 the IRS rolled out its annual tax time propaganda about "tax cheats". CNBC ran a feature on these scare tactics[6]. The IRS claims that 15% of taxpayers "cheat" on their taxes, but they chase the big name, headline grabbing taxpayers. Wesley Snipes was an example they glamorized. They IRS alleged his "CPAs and Attorneys advised him". They didn't mention the fact that Mr. Snipes request for due process was wantonly ignored. The sad truth is that every tipped employee in this country that doesn't report 100% of their tips, "cheats". Because the IRS doesn't have the manpower and doesn't want the bad publicity of terrorizing food service employees, casino workers and grooming specialists they worked out a compromise (during the Carter (D) years) and agreed to allow tipped employees to report 8% of their sales or all of the tips shown on credit cards whichever is higher. When the standard tip remains 15%-20% of the total bill, the 8% requirements implies it must be OK to leave out part of one's income? Former Treasury Secretary Geithner and Congressman Rangel left our part of their income. As we move closer to a cashless society all of those tipped employees will have to report more income.

The CBNC story also mentioned a $300 billion "tax gap", suggesting not all taxes are collected. Peter Goldmark in a column for *Newsday* in March, 2010 said "….the IRS estimate of the gap between taxes paid and taxes owed ----and it is north of $300 billion…" David Cay Johnson, a reporter for the NY Times put the number at $200 billion about fifteen years ago. Even with the IRS's Gestapo like powers the number

---

[6]   CNBC, January 7, 2012 "American Tax Cheats"

continues to climb, though the value of a dollar declines. The obvious question is, is it just hype to get their budget increased or is the system collapsing within itself?

Unfortunately CNBC wasn't intellectually honest enough to talk about the waste, fraud and corruption present in the government (at least 25% or $900 billion) and the "tax gap" pales in comparison. Likely, if everyone paid all the taxes they owe, the government would just have more money to waste.

This feature also demonized as a tax cheat and law breaker those who dare to take their money out of the country. The government views those who desire their right to privacy and the protection of their assets, from vulture lawyers, gold diggers, slip and fall artists and the government, as lawbreakers. The government ignores the possibility that returns on investments could be higher elsewhere and the fact that other parts of the world offer more affordable retirement options (see International Living). Instead, the government is tough on crime because everybody's a terrorist. It seems the IRS has adopted the instructions of "Deep Throat" (the Watergate informant), "follow the money".

I believe Cuba will be the next financial haven in the Western Hemisphere once the Castro regime is gone, and then there will be a giant sucking sound of money leaving this country. Cuba could become the gambling mecca of the Western Hemisphere as it was 60 years ago. Certainly the IRS is planning ahead to embarrass and demonize you now before it happens.

When Congressman Ron Paul campaigned for President in 2012 he made the point during a debate hosted by CNN, that fences aren't always intended to keep people/things out. Sometimes they are about keeping people/things in. His point was that we live in a world where relocating yourself and your assets is relatively easy. Because of this ease the government has now imposed a 30% tax on any amounts over $50,000 transferred out of the country and is extorting 33% of your wealth if you want to expatriate and live somewhere else in the world. Remember this is wealth that was earned legally and has already been taxed, but when governments become desperate, it make promises they can never keep and devalues the currency they have to trot out the "soak the rich mentality". Wealthy people from all over the world do have options about where they live and many countries will welcome Yankee Dollars with open arms.

Currently, some Washington bureaucrat has coined the term "economic patriotism" as though taking your money out of the country for privacy and asset protection is not patriotic. If you're thinking about starting a business you might want to ask yourself if it has to be based in the US. In today's electronic age it may be possible to do business from the moon. Keeping your money outside the country right from the get go might be a good idea. Eduardo Saverin, the co-founder of Facebook realized it and gave up his U.S. citizenship prior to the company's IPO.

CHAPTER TWO

SOCIAL ENGINEERING

Getting people to do what they normally do anyway, albeit a little sooner, should not be rewarded by a tax break. Most of the behavior the government, thru the tax code, wants people to engage in is probably intelligent, necessary, would save money or fill some need in their life. Politicians just want to prod you into spending sooner so they can take credit for how the spending stimulated the economy. Indeed, the economy can always stand all the stimulation it can get, just not from the government. Ultimately, these actions point to politicians' desire to buy votes.

Finding even one government program or tax benefit that started out as "temporary" but eventually expired proves a difficult task. [7] Perhaps even more difficult to find is program that cost exactly what the government said it would, did what it was supposed to do, in the time is was supposed to, and benefitted the people it was designed to without being overstaffed by unionized paycheck stealing bureaucrats. The FHA is in dire financial trouble yet the government does not hold anyone accountable (i.e. gets jailed, fired or replaced) for it. The same goes for the VA and the IRS.

---

[7] *Lies the Government Told You* by Andrew Napolitano, 2010, Thomas Nelson, Inc. publisher

Several tax breaks constitute the government's efforts to engineer society. These tend to affect middle class taxpayers regardless of whether they are an employee, independent contractor or businessman.

The most overhyped deduction is the <u>mortgage interest deduction</u>. Politicians and bureaucrats mistakenly believe that writing off the interest that one pays on the mortgage on their home will encourage home ownership. For those who were/are "under water" with their mortgage, have stopped paying their mortgage, lost their home or can't get a loan now to buy one even though prices and interest rates are cheap, the deduction obviously didn't work. The recent mortgage collapse showed us that the government was giving houses to people who couldn't afford them, and even with little or no down payment and a tax deduction for the interest they may have paid, they still could not afford the mortgage.

During the Clinton years, Treasury Secretary Robert Rubin appeared on the Sunday morning talk shows (during the tax filing season) to discuss "tax reform". He emphasized that in any discussions about "tax reform" Congress had to protect the sanctity of the mortgage interest deduction or people would not buy homes. The following day I had six clients come into my office to have their taxes done, five of whom were real estate agents and one was a real estate broker. I asked each of them how many times "did the deductibility of the buyer's mortgage interest" play a role in a prospective buyer's decision. All 6 of them looked at me like I was crazy. I then told them the story and they told me that most of their buyers paid cash so the issue was moot. In recent years, two of my children bought a house and neither one of viewed the mortgage interest as a critical part of the process. According to Treasury statistics only about one quarter of filers use the deduction. The "cost" to the Treasury was alleged to be $70 billion in 2013 (according to the Joint Committee on Taxation). Yet the money for those mortgages comes from FHA, Fannie Mae or Freddie Mac (i.e. the government/taxpayers) anyway.

The only way to "deduct" the mortgage interest paid is if one has certain itemized deductions and files a Schedule A with their income tax return. The tax code also offers the "standard deduction", an amount one can deduct from their income in computing what the government calls "taxable income" even if one didn't have a mortgage, donate to charity, pay property taxes or have unusual medical bills. Over the past 30 years Congress has raised that number so that for 2015 it now stands at $12,600 for a couple/$6300 for a single person. Unless a couple has a $200,000 mortgage with an interest rate of 5% or more they may not be able to itemize their deductions. The obvious question becomes "then what good does the mortgage interest deduction do"? While statistics suggest the median (middle ground) price of a home in the country today hovers around $200,000, if a person can't afford the payment, insurance, taxes, utilities, upkeep, the cost of commuting to work (assuming you liked the neighborhood, schools system, shopping amenities, color, layout and age), what difference does the mortgage interest deduction make? People don't make a bad deal simply because some vote seeking politician wants to hype this tax deduction?

Currently interest rates are below 5% and lots of properties can be bought right now for less than $200,000. However mortgages demand decent credit scores, a down payment and proof the buyer can make the payments. What then is the real benefit of this "mortgage interest deduction" and why has it become an impediment to real tax reform?

As an example, if your "itemized" deductions exceed the standard deduction the "tax savings or tax benefit" (cost to the Treasury) is simply the excess multiplied by one's tax rate, which for most working middle class couples/homeowners is either 15% or 25%. Let's assume this taxpayer is married, has a 5% mortgage with a balance of $180,000, during the first year of the mortgage and that the taxpayers had the mortgage from the 1st of January. (Any other scenario results in less interest paid that can be included in the itemization of the deductions and diminishes the net results).

Five percent of $180,000 is $9,000. It's quite obvious that number is less than the standard deduction and the taxpayer(s) is already borderline as to actually benefitting from this sacred "tax loophole". The lender may have assessed you some fees that can be added to the interest deduction and maybe the person paid their property taxes before December 31st just to get them in the mix. On a $200,000 house property taxes may be between 1 and 1 1/2%. Let's say $3,000. Additionally, the owner may be paying the mortgage insurance premium if he got a low down payment loan. Let's also assume this person generously gives $50 a week to his church, and was healthy and insurance takes care of your medical expenses. All of those available itemized deductions come to about $16,000 to $17,000 dollars. After deducting the standard $12,600 (2015) from that amount the tax deduction is $3,400 to $4,400. Assuming this person/couple is in the 15% Income tax bracket (under $60K of income) his/their "tax savings" is between $600 and $700 dollars. That probably won't even make one month's house payment and unless the price of gas stays down the oil companies will get it all. If this person is in the 25% tax bracket his "tax savings" would be between $1,100 and $1,350, and it's not entirely attributable to the mortgage interest deduction.

Every year that a mortgage is paid down, the interest deduction goes down, and the owner will no longer have those one time loan costs after the first year. With an adjustable rate loan which may actually go down even less interest is paid. The mortgage interest deduction has an even smaller benefit. This owner put $20,000 out of his pocket as a down payment on the house, went $180,000 in debt and now has to cut grass, patch the roof, paint it every so often, maintain the pool and clean up after the neighbor's dog to save $600 to $1,350? That's $12 to $25 *per week*, an amount that could be equaled through clipping coupons, turning in aluminum cans, cutting down on cigarettes or reducing your gas consumption. If you're single your "tax benefit" would be an extra 15% to 25% of $10,000 or about $1,500 to $2,500 if you bought that same $200,000 house a married couple did. That' still only an extra $30 to $50 a week.

Clearly, the argument supporting the mortgage interest deduction is a fallacy. With housing prices going up and "free money", any mortgage less than $300,000 with an interest rate less than 4% and less than a full twelve months' worth of payments will not result in any meaningful "tax benefit".

Those fortunate enough to belong to the 1% that the "occupy crowd" so fondly demonizes also belong to the top tax bracket where some benefit from the "mortgage interest deduction" can be seen. However, those who can afford to buy a home with a seven figure price tag likely don't make a decision to buy such a home because of the mortgage interest deduction. Those houses weren't exempt from the recent housing bubble, and for those people the amount of their "mortgage interest deduction" is limited to the interest on the first $1 million of the mortgage per year anyway. Real tax reform will save homeowners more money than anything gained from the interest on a mortgage.

A column (Youngstown, Oh. Vindicator) in January, 2012 authored by the local homebuilders association in Mahoning County ballyhooed the need to "save my mortgage interest deduction". They even had a website with that name. I wanted to call them up and ask "are you brain dead?" The cost of going to work to create the income stream to make the mortgage payments was climbing every day and they are concerned about a questionable tax deduction with suspect benefits. Killing the income tax and going to a consumption based tax would spur home buying, real estate investing and they want to protect a tax deduction that's part of a corrupt system. Why?

The second most over-hyped deduction/tax break is the <u>charitable donation deduction</u>. FACT: Christian people do not donate to worthy causes and needy people because it's "tax deductible". The disasters of the last decade in Indonesia, Haiti, Alabama, Missouri, New Jersey, New York, Oklahoma and other storm ravaged area are obvious examples. The idea, proffered by charities that donations will diminish if they aren't deductible is another fallacy. For the very wealthy, a tax deduction recoups some of their generosity but government has limited the amount of charitable donations that can be deducted by wealthy people. Do they therefore "limit" what they donate? Why should the tax code stifle generosity? As with the mortgage interest deduction the charitable donations deduction for lower and middle class people is available only if you exceed the standard deduction amount. Unless you tithe or are extremely generous don't expect to receive much of a tax benefit from Uncle Sam.

Faith based organizations deliver better services at a lower cost than any government agency. An intelligent option to effectively helping people in need is to scrap the income tax and let people donate to the charities/causes of their choice. It would also eliminate all the phoney foundations that have questionable operations. If public moneys are needed let the local communities vote on it, raise it and monitor it. Who better to watch the public's money and the results than those closest to it? The farther the money moves away from the people it was stolen from the less accountability and more waste and inefficiency there is.

Davy Crockett, while serving in Congress, voicing his opposition to a government charitable act said, "We have the right to, as individuals, to give away as much of our own money as we please in charity; but as members of Congress we have no right to appropriate a dollar of public money".[8] That sentiment was given to him by a constituent, Horatio Bunce while traveling his district.

If the federal government was actually sincere about helping the poor they could get rid of all the paycheck stealing bureaucrats on the government dole and give that money as block grants with no strings attached to the Red Cross, United Way, Jewish Relief Fund, Catholic Relief Fund, or a myriad of other charities, Davy Crockett's comment notwithstanding.

March 18, 2011 article in the Wall Street Journal talked about "itemized deductions" and offered the following data regarding those deductions at various income levels from poor to middle class. The claimed amounts

---

[8]   Warren,(OH) Tribune, Jan. 5, 2010 "Davy Crocket was correct….", Editorial by Stephanie McKnight

were the average for the income levels. My personal opinion is they are grossly in error.

Income	Medical	Taxes	Mortgage Interest	Charitable	Total
$15,000-$30,000	7,074	3,147	9,245	2,024	21,490
$30,000-$50,000	6,153	3,830	9,055	2,189	21,227
$50,000-$100,000	7,102	6,050	10,659	2,693	26,504

The article did not suggest where these people lived, their age, marital status, whether they had children or if they were employed or retired. Therefore I place very little stock in them, but am going to give the WSJ the benefit of having wasted the ink to offer these observations:

a) Anyone with an income of $30,000 or less in any year who files a tax return itemizing $21,490 of deductions should expect a knock on your door by the IRS. Regardless age and where one lives the IRS will take at least 7.65% (5.65% in 2012) of one's paycheck for the giant Ponzi scheme and the Medi-scare program. That's about $2,000 for $30K of income to $1,000 for $15K of income which that leaves you $6,510 per year or about $125 per week to buy groceries and gas, pay property insurance, maybe make a car payment, pay for a cell phone, internet and cable TV. Anyone who can accomplish this on $30,000 should be writing a book. *"How to Live on $30K a year and not go to jail"* might be an appropriate title. The other two possibilities could be a person is a walking bankruptcy and have maxed out your credit cards or is seriously ill and tapped out savings and/or retirement funds. All of those scenarios are aberrations and not typical costs of living.

Without any of these deductions a single taxpayer would pay about $3,000 in federal tax, $1,600 as a couple and nothing for a couple with a child. So how much of a "tax benefit" are you getting from being poor, broke, and destitute but owning your own home? In every one of those scenarios the mortgage interest in less than the standard deduction for a married couple and only slightly above that of a single person. Even when adding in the taxes (some of which could have been state or city income taxes) you barely exceed the magic number. No meaningful tax benefits exist without generous donations and catastrophic medical bills.

b) The medical expenses and the donations are about the same no matter which income bracket you fall into. It's surprising that even with the "tax deduction" for charitable donations people who make more money don't give more. Maybe they're giving it to their child's orthodontist or their manicurist.

A third example of social engineering was the institution of what I affectionately called the "poverty credit". The government calls it the "earned income tax credit". In the 1970's the federal government came to the realization that handing out unemployment checks served a double whammy, a) they could no longer confiscate money from the person out of work and b) it gave them somebody else's (taxpayers') money to soften their financial dilemma. When you pay somebody to do nothing they are going to do all the nothing they can for as long as they can. Most recently it was 99 weeks. Maybe it's time to have a bumper sticker quoting St. Paul (2nd Thessalonians 3:10) where he says if you don't work you don't eat.

When the United Auto Workers went after a "guaranteed annual wage" back in the 1970's they destroyed the incentive to work. Even high school graduates realized that getting 80% of your pay for doing nothing beat the heck out of working for 100%. They could go fishing, boating, hunting, golfing, skiing or travel and get paid for it. In the beginning the unemployment benefits weren't even subject to the income tax. It got so bad that the older seniority workers woke up to the fact that instead of being thankful they had a job they wanted the right to sit on their butts and get paid and let the newer/younger workers work.

The only negative was that they had to go back to work once they exhausted all their benefits. It took most of 30 plus years, but those chickens came home to roost and GM and Chrysler went bankrupt and a lot of auto industry jobs left the country. Automation and foreign competition is replacing the unionized autoworker.

The EIC is a refundable tax credit (you get a check) that was originally 10% of your EARNED income, if you had a dependent child. Now childless singles and couples under 65 may qualify. At first it only applied to a maximum income of $6,000 and phased out at $10,000. Over the years those amounts have increased to $22,000 and $50,000 (thanks to the government devaluing the dollar). While encouraging people to become gainfully employed, Congress did not consider that going to work usually required transportation and other related costs. Walking, bicycling and buses are certainly options in some areas but most people want the freedom and flexibility to come and go. This new incentive to go to work didn't always outweigh the costs.

In the case of working mothers or single parents, daycare or child care was also a necessity. Once a person analyzed his pay after taxes and the cost of collecting it, he saw that the EIC wasn't a good enough reason to go to work. Giving up rent subsidies, food stamps, free medical care and school lunches proved unrealistic. I never met a person who went to work just because he/she got an EIC. I did do tax returns for people who by happenstance got an EIC payment but would rather have been gainfully employed. Now when any alternative to the present tax system or "tax reform" is discussed it has to deal with the spin, (targeted at moochers) that reform will take it away. Any serious tax reform plan will do that. The people who promote the Fair Tax recognized that and have included a "pre-bate" in their plan to counter that argument. It basically gives poor people a check every month. (Once you give the moochers money to buy their vote it's impossible to take it back). Since the people who qualified for EIC payments still had money stolen from their check to subsidize the giant Ponzi scheme and the government health care system for senior citizens, whose money were they getting back? They were actually getting free social security coverage for any year they qualified for the EIC. How can the Social Security system not being going broke when people get free benefits? That wasn't part of the original program.

Fraud finds its way into every government program. The IRS processes a vast number of fraudulent returns with fraudulent dependents and billions of dollars lost because they didn't verify names, addresses, dependents and social security numbers before they gave out checks. The age of electronic filing made it even easier.

A February, 2011 article in the Warren (OH) Tribune Chronicle was captioned "IRS isn't stopping tax credits". The story begins by saying that "More than $10 billion a year in tax credits for low-income families go to people who don't qualify for them, and the IRS isn't doing enough to stop them". This news media picked up the story again in 2013. The program may have been a great headline grabber in 1976 and a great vote buying scheme but it did nothing to increase employment or reduce the budget deficits.

Fourth, on my list of social engineering gimmicks passed by Congress concerns the child care tax credit. In response to working parents (mostly single mothers) who complained about having to pay for day care or child care, Congress enacted the Child Care Tax Credit. It was designed to provide a subsidy to parents who had pre-school age children or school age children who needed supervision after school. Again this was a well-intended program that was initially wrought with problems. First, a lot of babysitters were paid in cash and there were no records or receipts to document the amounts claimed. Second, the provider usually forgot to declare the money (kind of like our former Treasury Secretary) as income. Third, some of the providers were family members who had other benefits (SSI, WC, unemployment) and weren't supposed to have earnings. Fourth, the credit was usually 20% of the amount paid the provider and did little to defray the actual cost of the child care. For those at the bottom of the income scale the credit could be as much as 30% of daycare costs, but still not much consolation. For those who made minimum wage it didn't help you at all. It finally dawned on the IRS that they were not getting a giant Ponzi scheme contribution from the at home childcare providers or from the "employer" parents.

Eventually the IRS demanded social security numbers for all providers be listed on the tax return of the person claiming the credit and insisted that the provider give the parent(s) a statement of what they actually paid the provider (what happened to personal responsibility and keeping your own records?). While these "reforms" may have stopped some of the billions lost with this program it did nothing to add to the employment rolls. In some cases I proved to women that they should stay home and that they would lose money going to work. As I mentioned in the earlier EIC discussion the net benefit analysis of going to some entry level job doesn't justify going to work. Employers concerned about retaining the most talented employees have started providing free day care to attract them.

Going to work is something 99% of us probably have to do some time in our lives, but replacing the tax system offers a much more intelligent solution that will encourage business development and employment not another tax credit/vote buying scheme.

Number five on my list of social engineering centers on the <u>retirement incentives</u>. While planning for your later years and retirement shows signs of accepting personal responsibility for one's own future far too many people don't have enough to live on when they reach that point in their life. The giant Ponzi scheme (affectionately called "social security") has been the primary component of most people's retirement income. Hopefully some kind of pension plan from all their years of employment also contributes to it. Sadly, however, many have to continue to work some part time or freelance job to make ends meet. Who expected $4-$5 gas when they planned to retire or double digit increases in health care costs? Or rising deductibles??

Knowing that the social "security" Ponzi scheme was being exposed and is broke, the government decided to encourage people to take care of their own retirement. They knew that every uptick in life expectancy just aggravates the unfunded liability problem social security faces.

As part of their desire to "encourage" this behavior the government created Individual Retirement Accounts, Simplified Employee Plans and 401K/403B plans and made contributions to these type of accounts "tax deductible" and the earnings "tax deferred". These provide yet another example of the government's "if you do this we will give you a tax break" mentality. However, the government didn't want it to be too attractive so they set limitations and conditions for setting up one of these accounts. It was a windfall to the banks, brokerage houses and insurance companies for all their campaign donations. A former chairman of the Senate Finance Committee William Roth, wanted one of the accounts named after him.

Originally a person could only contribute $2,000 to a self-directed retirement account. Of course that was when $2,000 actually bought something. Now the limit is $5,000. There are also restrictions based on income, or other retirement plans, and one's age. Until recently there were even restrictions on what one could invest their money in. All of these restrictions did more harm than good and when people in the lower tax brackets realized that investing, contributing or otherwise tying up their money only saved them $300 - $500 in taxes they balked. It did benefit those who could basically move money from one pocket (an existing savings or investment account) and move it to the other pocket (an IRA etc.) and get a tax deduction. However, for those in the upper tax brackets the aforementioned restrictions probably negated being able to set up an IRA. It has not taken any of the pressure off the giant Ponzi scheme and has now started a long overdue movement to make paying into that program voluntary as was the original intention of Congress. A well-intended case of social engineering that didn't produce the desired benefits.

A recent story on *TheHill.com* by Bernie Becker suggested the Obama administration has decided anyone who has money in one of these types of accounts is well off and politicians want to attack the moneys in those retirement or tax deferred programs so they can continue to finance the free stuff they give to the moochers who vote for them. Congress thinks people with retirement accounts shouldn't have that money sitting outside the reach of the IRS. The real advantage to these accounts was the *tax free* accumulation of money earned off the investments. Ending the income tax would accomplish the same thing. The market crash in 2008 certainly had many people worried. Luckily the Department of Labor has expanded acceptable alternatives to Wall Street investments for IRA accounts and if one can "beat the street" a person can have quite a nest egg and won't have to count solely on the Ponzi scheme for their retirement.

Number six and seven on my list that scream social engineering are the "cash for clunkers" program and the first time home buyer tax credit. Cash for clunkers was not a true tax loophole program but both were designed to stimulate the economy, used taxpayer money to encourage a behavior the government wanted since GM and Chrysler were in bankruptcy, and the housing, real estate and construction markets were dead. Like every other giveaway program they may have been well intended but had no real effect on the economy. With 70% of GM workers outside the U.S. whose jobs did they save? People who may have needed a car may have accelerated that purchase but they didn't buy just to get a check and they did not require a participant to buy an American-made car. The rebate process was much slower than hyped and when it was all over car sales went back to being flat. The Toyota recall at the time cast doubt on the safety of all cars and choked off sales again.

As is the case with all tax write-offs, credits, deductions and loopholes abuse crept into the home buyer program. People who could not afford to make payments or come up with a down payment weren't going to buy just because they could get a check. The government had to extend the deadline because buyers who could afford to pick up a bargain couldn't close fast enough due to the government imposed restrictions after the collapse of Fannie and Freddie. Once the program ended sales slid again because qualified buyers (who were going to buy anyway) had simply accelerated their purchases. It was a sale that was going to happen sooner or later, the government just wanted to try to make it sooner. But in their infinite idiocy the IRS gave away $27 million dollars in erroneous refunds to tax-filers, including $9 million to 1,300 PRISON INMATES[9], some of whom were serving life sentences. Of those receiving erroneous refunds 87 were IRS employees. No bureaucrats went to jail. What part of that $27M could have resulted in lower taxes or been given to save your home? How many small businesses could they have funded with $27M?

Number eight on the list deals with <u>education</u>, though the government has never truly been in favor of educating the masses. Brainwashing yes, educating NO. If you don't believe that read *"The Deliberate Dumbing-Down of America"* by Charlotte Thomson Iserbyt (1999). Yes, she said deliberate. Nobody believes in the need for an education than I do. I don't agree with the way it's funded or with government intervention. An educated electorate threatens every sitting member of Congress either for what they did or for what they didn't do.

Under pressure from lobbyists (i.e. shakedowns for tax breaks) Congress established perks for college students. A tax credit for part of the cost of attending college in the first two years of a four year program and a tax deduction for the interest paid on a student loan were enacted. College students did not have to itemize this particular interest on Schedule A to get the deduction since most of them don't make much money and don't itemize. Parents footing the bill of a dependent child can use the tax credit, but the interest deduction stayed with the student.

Since most full time students have limited income while trying to further their education, the interest deduction provides nice press releases but offers little value. Many loans have the interest deferred until after

---

[9] Youngstown Vindicator, June 24, 2010 "1300 Inmates get $9M tax break", Associated Press

graduation. Even if students earn income it is very unlikely their tax bracket is in excess of 15% or 25% and spending a dollar that returns only 15 (or 25) cents doesn't make much sense. For those students who may be working full time and pursuing their studies in the evenings, on weekends or on line the deduction may be a tiny subsidy but grants, scholarships, employer reimbursements, car- pooling or living at home are much more intelligent approach and subsidy. I'd be much more concerned about $4-$5 gas than some measly tax deduction. Once a person completes their studies, has a diploma and enormous student debt, a 15% tax deduction for the interest he or she probably can't pay anyway isn't going hasten paying off the debt. In my opinion the cost of that education is double what it should be because of all the government programs. A young man who was part of a panel discussion about college costs on a talk show, that I came upon while channel surfing, was asked why the colleges and universities charged so much. His answer was quote "because they can!" When they know the student isn't paying up front for the cost of his/her education and the money is coming from taxpayer grants and loans they simply inflate the costs and are never held accountable.

The other "tax benefit" to encourage education is a tax credit of $2,500 (maximum) for expenses incurred during the first two years of a college education. Students don't have to maintain a passing grade to get the credit they just need money. It does not bring down the cost of a college education. In fact any benefit a student may have gained has long since been wiped out by the decline in the purchasing power of a dollar and outrageous price of books. And now all the kids who went to college and can't find a job want the government to forgive, forget, or otherwise ignore the loans they have to repay. Demonstrating on Wall Street will not solve the problem. Go picket the IRS office in Washington, elect a whole new Congress and demand a new tax system.

I doubt seriously if these "tax breaks" made it easier or more affordable to get an education. It simply panders to lobbyists and gets press clippings for allegedly helping middle class parents or poor students. Instead we should focus on bringing down the cost of education, first by abolishing the Department of Education; second by stopping all government subsidies; third by encouraging students to working their way through school, attending in-state schools, and living at home; fourth, stop throwing away/changing text books after one quarter or semester; and fifth, eliminating the present income tax system and let people have the means to get the education of their own choosing before being plundered by an antiquated system. Get over the concept that the government (other people's tax money) owes you a free education.

Number nine on the list of social engineering relates to energy credits. Since the Nixon years the country has been on an agenda to save energy. (In my opinion it was a "save it now so we can charge you more for it later" mentality). Their solution again, tinker with the tax code. In the 1970's the credits applied to insulation and repairs to homes that stop leaks and wasted energy. Now the hype focuses on "green energy" and anything that reduces dependence on fossil fuels. Obviously anything that saves energy saves people money. Why do people need a tax credit to engage in intelligent behavior? If politicians understood the true cost of carrying this abusive tax system we wouldn't need another government give away. I believe the technology has long since existed to allow cars to routinely get 60 MPG and last longer, but then auto companies and oil companies wouldn't sell as many cars or as much oil, though prices of both would drop.

Number ten is a tax deduction that epitomizes social engineering. It's the so called "capital gains tax". There is no capital gains "tax", it's still a tax on income, merely a specified tax rate for the income earned from what is defined as investment by the tax code. When you give to moochers you have to offset it with incentives to the producers. The reason it appears oppressive is that the tax is a lump sum regardless of how low the regular tax rate is. Capital gains used to be 60% exempt from the income tax, then 50% exempt, then taxed at a flat rate of 20% and now 15%. It was to encourage investment, as though making money wasn't enough of an incentive. While it probably benefitted rich people, it is available to middle class taxpayers who dabbled in the stock market and make some real estate investments. It seems some politicians realized they actually needed private sector investments to stimulate the economy. However, even with the cheaper rate the stock market still crashed, the housing bubble burst, and real unemployment is unacceptably high

Business incentive. Even though they tend to demonize corporations and businesses Congress enacted the "Section 179 deduction". It allows the purchaser of business equipment to expense the cost of that equipment in the year of purchase even if it's done at the 11th hour as opposed to depreciating the item over multiple years. While it may help the business for the current year it may actually be better to estimate the total benefits before making a decision. Sadly this write off didn't prevent the recent economic downturn. Businesses still need customers and less government interference much more than they need tax gimmicks.

A myriad of special breaks in the tax code for corporations and businesses (i.e. corporate jets, offshore subsidiaries, the oil depletion allowance, etc.) are "perfectly legal" but are also no reason to keep the system. Tax credits for hiring felons, vets, the long term unemployed, disabled Americans, students etc. is also a form of social engineering enacted to help businesses. The federal government does not create jobs, just grief and aggravation so it has to "tinker with the tax code" and give incentives to the same businesses it demonizes to help solve the problems it created. None of this social engineering or tax tinkering can justify keeping the present system when so many abuse the system.

Corporations consider taxes just another cost of doing business and include it in the price they charge the consumers for their product. They really don't care what corporate tax rates are because they don't pay them anyway. You the consumer pay them in the form of higher prices.

According to Scott Klinger an associate fellow at the Institute for Policy Studies[10].. American corporations have stashed more than $1.4 trillion

---

offshore. While some of this loot is derived from U.S. corporations selling goods and services to people abroad, much of it is reaped from accounting tricks. For example, a drug company will register parent companies in tax haven nations like Luxembourg or the Netherlands, and charge enormous fees". All of which are "perfectly legal". (You can read a book by the same title also by David Cay Johnson). Again, who had control of Congress from 2006 until 2010? I wonder how many of those "evil" corporations paid for their campaigns. These companies are not doing anything illegal, so the government chooses to demonize them rather than change the law. Abolishing the income tax would completely take the wind out of their sails.

CONCLUSION: The present system has questionable origins, is a disaster, is not fair (whatever that is), has outlived any usefulness ever intended, doesn't need any more tinkering, cannot be reformed and must be replaced. Every former and sitting member of Congress whose name is not on a bill to abolish the income tax and the IRS should be removed from office.

CHAPTER THREE

MY OWN EXPERIENCES

In 1997 I read an article from *Media Bypass Magazine* authored by a couple (that I later spoke with) doing research for an Alabama attorney regarding the "roots" of the IRS. The article was styled as a letter to Margaret Richardson, the IRS Commissioner at that time. It raised serious questions about where one could find any law that created an agency known as the Internal Revenue Service. The truth is, there is none, which was the point of the article. Ms. Richardson did not respond to the letter, and actually resigned before her term expired. The article brought out the fact that what is now the "IRS" was a part of the Alcohol, Firearms and Tobacco Agency (ATF) that simply changed its name. You will see on the attached charts related to the structure of the U.S. Department of the Treasury the IRS is not listed on one, and a low level bureau on the other one. One will never see the letters "U.S." before the words "Department of the Treasury" on any notice generated by them. In the early part of this century the official instructions for making a payment for any balance due on a tax return were changed to say "make the check payable to the Department of the Treasury", no longer "Internal Revenue Service". It certainly adds credibility to what the authors portrayed.

Taxpayers should write their "Congress-critter" to ask for an explanation. If they were lucky enough to a response, it probably will contain some gobble-de-gook about an 1862 law that created something called the

"Bureau of Revenue" during the Civil War. What they won't tell you is that law was repealed as part of the General Compromise Act after the war.[11] So why all the secrecy? Don't these people know when and how they came into existence? Former Texas Congressman Dick Armey (R) had suggested he wanted to pull the IRS "out by its roots", if only they could be found. It's a safe assumption employees and investors of major corporations know its history.

No private corporation is supposed to have a name identical to that of a government agency, yet there is an entity in Nevada known as "Department of the Treasury-Internal Revenue Service"[12]. How can that be?? Could it be the government is lying to us? In 2016 a federal judge issued an injunction against the company after an attorney tried to "serve" something on the "IRS" at the Nevada address.

In my early years as a professional accountant I had a client come to my office who suggested he and his wife hadn't filed his taxes in a while. I asked how long was "awhile"? He said eight years, however both he and his wife were employees and had taxes withheld from their paychecks and received a W-2 form. Two things went through my mind, a) how did the IRS allow these people to go that long without filing because it's allegedly a crime not to file, and b) are these people for real or were they undercover IRS personnel trying to entrap someone?

Obviously in the 1970's the IRS computer system had some serious defects. The returns were relatively simple and the taxpayers actually overpaid their taxes most of the eight years. However, there is a three year statute of limitations to claim a refund and they lost out on the refunds from the oldest of the eight years.

Another of my former clients from the 1970's owned three low income housing projects. The IRS decided to audit them because at that time they were set up as limited partnerships which were thought to be abusive

---

[11] *How the Courts Constrain Tax Reform*, Bruce Bartlett, NY Times Jan 14, 2014

[12] Nevada Div. of Corporations

tax shelters. In those days the IRS actually respected the clients' right to designate a representative, i.e. a Power of Attorney. I made arrangements for the agent to come to my office and examine the clients' records. The lady who handled all of the books was meticulous to a fault and I had no concerns about any surprises. The IRS agent spent most of twenty-one days in my office. Two of the other tenants in the building wanted to know who my new employee was, since he had been there so long. When I told them the story they were surprised. The adjustment the agent wanted to make to so trivial it didn't generate any significant revenue for the IRS nor justify his time spent. Of course he was "just doing his job", but some jobs just don't need to be done.

My best friend in the accounting world was Alvin Hopkins, a CPA in Youngstown, Ohio. He passed away several years ago. One of Alvin's employees was a former IRS employee who had retired. The agent's most recent position, within the IRS, had been to train agents in how to conduct audits. He told Alvin and I he tried to instill in new agents three rules: a) if you find something that constitutes criminal fraud keep digging and refer the file to higher authorities; b) if the facts don't support criminal fraud keep digging to determine if civil penalties should be assessed, and c) if neither A or B apply get the hell out of there.

In the early 1980's before I moved to Florida one of the IRS agents that testified at my trial attacked a taxpayer before the taxpayer and I met. When the agent was all done he told the taxpayer that he may be wrong in the changes he proposed, but "how much money do you want to spend fighting me?" If any IRS agent had made a comment like that to one of my clients he'd probably be selling shoes today. A few years later after I met the client and heard the story, I agreed to look over what the agent had done. I had to tell the client that his records were not very good and he may owe the money. The agent had also punished the client for the state of his records by adding $9,000 of penalties and the related interest. I felt those were an obvious case of abuse and unnecessary. I researched the matter and we gave our information to a tax attorney who agreed with us. He filed an appeal and the client got the penalties and interest back. The client was shocked but felt vindicated.

In the mid 1980's after I had established a practice in Florida I had a client I thought was being abused by the IRS and I wrote a complaint letter calling them Gestapo agents. Now I call them terrorists. (BTW: the governor from Maine who called them the new Gestapo didn't need to apologize). The IRS employee who got the letter called my office, spoke with my secretary and told her the matter would be resolved in favor of the client. She also said if she ever started a business she'd hire me because I fight for my clients.

One of the more ridiculous idiocies of the tax system involved a lady who was originally from Eastern Europe and lived in Florida and was a US citizen. Her elderly father came to live with her in the last year of his life and when she filed her tax return she claimed him as a dependent since he was related to her, she supported him, he was with her over half the year, *but* was not a US Citizen. The IRS denied her the deduction. The "cost" to government would have been about $300, but they grabbed for the "letter of the law". (Yet we have 11 million illegals mooching off the Treasury today with no consequences.)

In the late 1990's I filed an appeal, on behalf of a client, with the Atlanta Service Center to an IRS demand for payment. I subsequently got a call from an IRS employee from the Memphis, Tennessee office. I questioned why she was calling me since the taxpayer lived in Florida and Atlanta was the center that Florida reported to. She told me Atlanta had a backlog and some of the cases were referred to Memphis. I told her I had serious doubts about whether the people in Atlanta were intellectually astute enough to handle the inquiries they got. She told me the people in Memphis wondered the same thing. The IRS had a bad habit of recruiting bodies, running them through a training class that should be called "the world according to the IRS", waving hands over their heads and sending them on their way. Their mission: "go forth and terrorize all nations."

In 1997 I was attacked twice by the IRS's Criminal Investigation Division over two former clients. One had always filed but didn't pay, the other owned a landscape business and the IRS alleged the client did business from his home as well as his business location. A friend who at one time operated a "hot-line" for callers with questions about taxes suggested I attend a seminar in Clearwater that was being hosted by Eddie Kahn. He thought Mr. Kahn may be able to offer some ideas on how to deal with IRS. Mr. Kahn stood in front of the audience and said he hadn't filed a tax return since 1979. My obvious reaction was why "wasn't he in jail" or did he know something the rest of us didn't? In both of the cases I got called to testify at a grand jury hearing but nothing else came of them.

As mentioned in chapter one, David Cay Johnson a writer for the NY Times did a column suggesting the IRS couldn't collect $200 billion a year it thought it was owed. At the time that would have been enough to balance the federal budget for one year. But it begs the question, "how and why do these people get away without paying?" and the corollary, "why am I paying if they're not?"

In 2001 an excerpt of a letter from the IRS to a taxpayer said 63 MILLION people (in 1996) didn't file a federal income tax return.[13] That was about 1 out of every 4 adults in the country at the time. Some of those non-filers may have actually died or were dying. Others high on drugs, suffering from illness, depressed over losing a job, recently divorced, or simply fed up supporting moochers. I'm sure that the number has gone up significantly during the recent depression. When he left the Commissioner's job in 2002 Charles Rossetti complained the IRS was losing the battle with tax protestors.

In 2001 while dealing with a penalty assessed against a client I received a phone call from the person in Atlanta who was handling the matter and was assured the taxpayer was correct and the file would be corrected. The lady asked if I had any other questions, and so I said "How much longer is the IRS going to be around?" The reason I asked the question

---

[13]   Freedom Law School website, IRS response letter

is that if 63 million people weren't filing a tax return why weren't those people in prison? Obviously we don't have the space to put them. The lady said "I hope five more years so I can retire". I found her choice of words interesting. Sadly the IRS is still here.

My co-defendant, Eddie Kahn, had a visit in 2001 from the Treasury Inspector General for Tax Administration's (TIGTA) office in response to twelve hundred complaints American Rights Litigators had filed (as provided for by section 1203 of the IRS Reform and Restructuring Act of 1998) against IRS personnel for violating taxpayers' rights. The agents that were investigating the matter were only interested in determining if the IRS was in compliance with the Fair Debt Collection Act. That was their "hot button". They ignored all of the other constitutional and due process issues Mr. Kahn's organization had raised, though it would seem even the IRS has to comply with some laws.

With the passage of two Taxpayer Bills of Rights and the IRS Reform and Restructuring Act of 1998 IRS employees were supposed to give taxpayer's their name and ID number whenever they contacted a taxpayer. I think they have stopped doing it even though the law has never repealed. It seems as recently as fifteen years the IRS had a habit of using aliases and mechanically signing names of people who didn't really exist. At one time the name "W. H. Gregory" was "signed" as the Head of the Automated Collection Service (ACS) in Atlanta. In reality "W. H. Gregory" didn't exist. I remember calling the IRS's "800" number in response to a letter a client received with that "signature". I asked to speak to "W.H. Gregory". The woman who answered said "Oh, I can take that call". She did resolve the inquiry favorably and I never gave it a thought, but later learned of their ruse.

At one time the IRS actually had a hotline for taxpayer's to call and ask a question. I thought of it as the "fox guarding the hen house" and was astounded that any taxpayer would call those people and expect to get a response that benefitted them. Clients would come to my office and say "I called the IRS...." To which I'd say, "Then why are you talking to me?" The obvious answer was they weren't happy with what the IRS told them, or didn't tell them. The hotline was eventually discontinued after, when audited by the Government Accounting Office (GAO), the IRS was found to have given out erroneous information two out of every three times they responded.

A common myth about income taxes is that taxpayers should get a refund every year. Not so fast. Taxpayers should always owe the government a little and make them wait for it until the very last minute, and later if possible. The politicians are just going to squander it. Getting any refund over a couple hundred dollars screams poor money management. I realize it's a common malady in this world thanks to government schools and the instant gratification society we live in, but all people are doing is making the government an interest free loan. Has anyone ever been given an interest free government backed mortgage, SBA loan or a student loan? Did anyone ever get an interest free car loan from a government owned bank? A military credit union? So why are taxpayers giving the government free money?

There are two options people should consider if you are habitually getting large refunds. First, increase the amount one puts into their 401K plan, 403B, or start an IRA, and have that deducted from their check. In either case people never see the money and won't really miss it. Many employers match the employee's contributions to 401K plans. Second, open an interest bearing account at a local credit union and have money from your paycheck deposited into that account instead of the Treasury's account. Though the government may not pay you a dime in interest since they have been forced to deliberately manipulate interest rates to historic lows to keep the federal deficit from being worse. A dollar in interest on your money is better than a free loan to the government. In either case, the money will be under your control and if an emergency arises you have access to it without having to "throw down the plastic" and paying interest. When suggesting this to clients, I heard all the excuses: "if I can get to it, I'll just spend it", "it is how we go on vacation"; "it's how we pay the bills after Christmas", or "it's the only way I can save money". Those people have no money manage skills or self-control, will complain about what an abusive agency the IRS is and yet still they throw money at them and overpay them.

If during the year you have an event that you didn't expect (i.e. business failure, job loss, investment gone bad, a casualty loss etc.) employees should estimate the effect on their tax liability and fill out a new form (W-4) to reduce what their employer is deducting and put the money into one of the aforementioned accounts. Anyone making estimated payments should re-compute those as well.

Another myth is that people who get a refund don't believe they pay taxes. One of the other inmates I met while "on vacation", whom I'll call "M", suggested to me that he didn't pay taxes he a got a refund every year. "M" had a college degree, a $150,000/year job and was savvy enough to engage in an activity that got him a vacation at Club Fed yet didn't realize that every dollar confiscated from his check, bonuses or commissions for the income tax and the giant Ponzi scheme certainly meant HE PAID TAXES. He never gave a thought to what he left behind, just what pittance they gave back to him. How much of his money was wasted by the government never entered his mind. I could only shake my head. "M" also cashed out his 401K plan (without sound advice from a tax professional) to pay on his restitution. Unfortunately it didn't get him any extra time off, and he had a $100,000 tax bill and no income when he did get released.

MYTH: penalties are bad. Not true. Late paying, underestimating, late filing....where can anyone get a loan without an application, committee meeting, collateral and cheap interest? I never made estimated payments in my life. There is no law that requires it. There is possibly a "penalty" for not having done it, IF one owes money. If a person is hard pressed for money, the IRS's interest is cheap and without all the loan hoops to jump thru. Filing late may be unavoidable but is still cheaper than paying too much. Always file an extension when not sure. The IRS does make payment plans but they charge a fee (minimum $43) for the privilege. A person could simply send the IRS whatever they can afford on a weekly basis which the IRS will not refuse. The account will show activity which keeps the dogs at bay without filling out of forms, seeking approval or incurring extra charges.

For those who are being harassed by IRS collection employees don't buy the myth: federal income taxes can't be discharged in bankruptcy. If a person owes any large amount of money to the IRS for income tax, penalties and interest consult with an experienced bankruptcy attorney before doing anything. Some taxes are dischargeable within certain parameters. If they are not dischargeable they may be paid at the rate of 30 cents on the dollar over time. Do not get sucked in by the companies advertising to compromise your debt. They charge too much. Bankruptcy is cheaper and available to all. Most bankruptcy attorneys have a free initial consultation policy, take advantage of it.

There is a theory that suggests someone with a tax debt should consider paying it with a credit card and then discharging that debt in bankruptcy. It basically amounts to the same thing. However, there are waiting periods before a person can discharge the credit card debt. In the meantime an open federal tax lien on a credit file is just as bad as a bankruptcy.

It totally amazed me that an agency with Gestapo like powers would have to resort to farming out some of its collection activities to private collection agencies, but several years ago the IRS did just that.[14] At least people quivered when the IRS called. They just blow off private collections agencies. It seems that when you're not a legally authorized agency of the United States government you can't go into court and sue. In bankruptcy they still have to take a number and get in line behind secured creditors. They are slowly beginning to realize, "You can't get blood from a turnip" and the use of illegal liens, levies and seizures is being exposed. [15]

---

[14]   Amerian Jobs Creation Act created Code Sect. 6306, 8/23/06
[15]   Michigan Appeals Court, 2001

During my 35 years of practice I would fight for abused taxpayers regardless of how much money was involved. Abuse is abuse; though there were times when paying "the protection money" was the cheapest thing to do.

I think the government now has a serious problem collecting taxes under the present system, but wait until the Castro regime is gone and Cuba becomes the new financial haven of the Western Hemisphere. Cuba will thumb their nose at the IRS and the U.S. Government. I can only hope they will charge the U.S. and "arm and a leg" for keeping Gitmo open. From what I read the U.S. Navy needs that port for its submarine maneuvers since it's allegedly the only deep water port on this side of the Atlantic Ocean.

US Department of Treasury Organization Chart - Top Level

< US Gov org

Run OrgScope map of US Government

Download PDF of US Treasury org chart

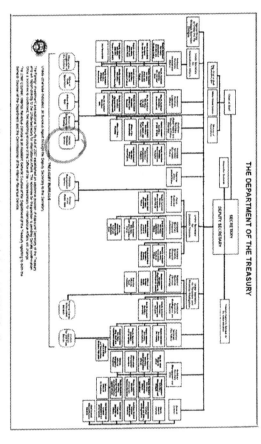

THE DEPARTMENT OF THE TREASURY

http://www.ustreas-gov/organization/org-chart-04242008.pdf
This no longer works

NOTE: Shortly after the new administration took office, the Treasury org chart was removed from the department's web site. As of February, 2010, the US Treasury Department has still not posted a chart, old or new

U.S. DEPARTMENT OF THE TREASURY

About

Organizational Structure

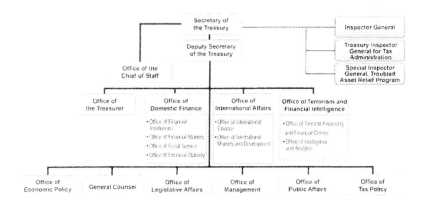

Treasury Officials
Biographies of the Treasury Leadership.

Bureaus
The Treasury Bureaus, such as the IRS and the US Mint, carry out specific operations.

Offices
The Treasury Offices headed by Assistant Secretaries and Under Secretaries.

Inspectors General
The three Inspectors General of the Treasury.

OPEN/GOV

CHAPTER FOUR

MORE TAX TINKERING

The government is stealing money from the citizenry in more ways than just the income tax and payroll tax. This is a list of what's been done in the last decade, per a column by Grover Norquist, the president of Americans for Tax Reform. Mr. Norquist is probably the lobbyist Liberals, Democrats, progressives hate the most because he understands waste.

1) Raised the federal excise tax on cigarette by 61 cents a pack (156%). (A regressive tax) (Footnote: Obama wants to raise it again)
2) Obamacare Individual Mandate Excise Tax (what a mouthful that one is). That's the one for NOT buying health insurance starting in 2014. (But it may be cheaper than the cost of insurance) (A regressive tax)
3) Obamacare Employer Mandate Tax. A $2,000 tax on employers who does not OFFER health insurance. (Only those with 50 or more employees) Lots of waivers?? Doesn't that hurt medium sized business??
4) A surcharge of 3.8% on investment income for higher income filers.
5) The "Cadillac" insurance plan tax. (Doesn't start until 2018)
6) Medicare payroll tax.
7) Medicine cabinet tax.

8) Early W/D penalty from HSAs. (A regressive tax)
9) FSA limit (Special needs kids). (Social engineering)
10) Tax on medical device manufacturers. (which they will pass on to consumers and Congress wants to repeal)
11) Itemized medical deduction deductible increase to 10%. (How does that help?)
12) Tax on Indoor Training Salons. Isn't that a middle class tax hike? A regressive tax?
13) Eliminate tax deduction for retiree RX coverage.
14) BC/BS tax hike. (which they will pass on)
15) $50K penalty on charitable hospitals that don't meet rules.
16) Tax on Innovator Drug Companies.
17) Tax on Health Insurers with $50M in profits.
18) Limit on Exec Comp for Health Care Companies. (There is already a limit on executive comp)
19) Reporting of insurance on W-2 form (Obama wants to tax health benefits-middle class tax hike). (A regressive tax)
20) Tax on a certain Bio-fuel. (A regressive tax)
21) IRS abuse opportunity if legal deductions and planning don't have "substance".

I'd say that's twenty-one more great reasons to abolish the current tax system since most of them hit the middle class in the form of higher prices.

I strongly support former Congressman Ron Paul's premise we can abolish the income tax and replace it with nothing, knowing the money collected by the income tax only covers the interest on the debt, what the government deems national defense and pensions for former federal employees[16] who created this mess.

"We all play a part in the deteriorating economy. We are all to blame every time we choose an imported, foreign made product over an American product. But, America will not create private sector jobs

---

[16]   Grace Commission Report, Jan. 1984

until our Government removes the costly burdens that are killing our companies and manufacturers. The Internal Revenue Service must also be abolished. And our Government must replace our tax-revenue scheme." (Former Congressman Jim Traficant (D-OH, the Review Newspaper/Oct. 2010)

Nobody on this planet wants to see an end to the income tax and the IRS more than I, not just because of their attacks on me but because I don't believe in the "Robin Hood" concept of taxation. I am vehemently opposed to any income tax based system even though I profited off of it for thirty five years. I believe the fruits of a man's labor must be held sacred.

Businessman Steve Forbes, former Congressman Texas Dick Armey and former Texas Governor Rick Perry seem to be like the idea of a "flat tax". In 1982 we had the closest thing to a flat-tax the country has seen since 1913. President Reagan pushed a bill thru a Democratic controlled Congress to cut all the tax brackets to two, 15% and 28%. At the time a married couple could earn about $100,000 (that's over $300,000 in 2015 dollars) and pay at most 21% of it in income tax. That was in addition to the Ponzi scheme and Medi-scare contributions which were collected on a maximum $32,400 at the time. The 21% rate by itself was hardly worth lying, cheating and getting involved with "tax shelter" investments. Unfortunately, Congress couldn't stop spending money like drunken sailors, and decided the rich could afford to pay more and the "flat tax" went out the window. ANY continuation of the income tax will always invite mischief and class warfare.

CHAPTER FIVE

THE SOLUTION

There is a solution to this madness, idiocy and out right financial slavery. Americans have been living under an oppressive tax system for over 100 years. Let's give sanctity to the fruits of a man's labor, try something different for 100 years and then compare. It's time to go to something that is simple, doesn't discourage the entrepreneurial spirit, doesn't require lawyers /accountants, doesn't chase money out of the country, doesn't foster tax sheltered transactions, phony foundations/charities, and isn't run by a bunch of terrorists. It's long past time for a consumption tax. It's simple, easy to administer, voluntary, puts the people in control of their money and takes power out of the hands of dirtbags, liars and power freaks.

Try to get your mind around the idea of leaving work every payday with your entire earnings in your hands (or deposited into your bank account), never again having to file a 1040 form, never having to live under the threat of an IRS audit, and paying if, when and how much one chooses. (Those who live in an area that has city or state income taxes wouldn't get 100% of their earnings). If you didn't stop reading this book after the introduction you may see the wisdom of such a system. The comment I get most from people I explain it to is "That's too simple it'll never pass!"

Instead of listening to liberal political hacks, like the MSNBC crowd, criticize the plan because the rich might not be paying their fair share (whatever that is) or the poor will be unduly burdened, I challenge everyone to look at their own personal situation and finances, do the math and decide which is the better system. Don't let anybody, including me, tell you what it's going to do (or not do) for you until you know the facts. Anyone who is part of the "moocher generation" and has to pay even $1 in tax will glamorize it as a tax increase. Those who want to continue the "Robin Hood" system will also dismiss it. What they neglect to tell people is that drug dealers are going to pay the tax when they spend their ill-gotten gains. People who conveniently forgot to report all their income will pay tax, as well as those who live in the underground economy.

There has been a movement in the country since the late 1990's to do away with the IRS, the personal income tax, the payroll tax, the corporate income tax and repeal the 16th amendment. Sadly the left wing media has refused to give it any attention and the right wing media has never developed a plan and educate the people to the benefits of such a system. "Tax reform proposals are the political equivalent of science fiction….. there are too many interests that believe their survival depends on tax preference.."[17] Tax reform doesn't garner enough rating points for the media to cover it. Scandals, mayhem, war and elections get a higher priority and generate more advertising dollars.

Americans for Fair Taxation, a Houston based organization, is promoting what is called "the Fair Tax", a national retail sales tax. The Fair Tax would replace the personal income tax, the corporate income tax and the giant Ponzi scheme. Herman Cain is a leading proponent of this plan but didn't have the political backing to promote it during his failed presidential run in 2012. AFT's website is www.fairtax.org. Before the 2014 elections the bill had seventy-five co-sponsors in the House and eight in the Senate. Sadly none of them are Democrats, though the original bill had a Democrat (Colin Peterson, MN) and a Republican (John Linder, GA) as its co-sponsors. Mr. Linder has since left Congress.

---

[17]   *Tax reform is a fairy tale*, Doyle McManus, LA Times, Nov. 8, 2011

Without class warfare and blaming the rich for not paying their fair share to many Democrats can't support real tax reform.

In order to promote this bill, and vote for it, your Congress-critters have to ignore the #1 reason why the present system has festered so long, that being to shakedown potential donors for money and punishing your enemies. In other words my re-election is more important than what's good for the people. Peter Sweitzer has a book on this very subject that validates my point.[18] I'll discuss this more in the third part of this book.

The Fair Tax organization spent twenty million dollars on research related to the Fair Tax and concluded that 23% is the rate that has to be collected on each sale at the retail level to make it "revenue neutral". I'm not sure that when the government wastes at the very least one quarter of what they spend why do we need neutrality? The 23% tax will be included in the cost of the price shown on the item being purchased. The plan only collects the tax on <u>new</u> goods and services. Opponents of this plan call it a 30% sales tax since all other state or local sales taxes are added on to the price of the product or service being purchased. While one can argue all day over the percentage, the fact is out of every $100 a customer spends on taxable items the federal government is going to get $23. Everybody who pays is going to pay the same rate. Those below poverty, will pay nothing. Because government spending is a major contributor to the decrease in the value of the dollar it may be a good idea to redefine poverty and adjust it for inflation.

The United States, in 2013, had a $15 trillion dollar economy. That does not include all the illegal activities. If half of that amount were transactions subject to the "Fair Tax" the government would collect $1.725 trillion dollars which is about what the income and payroll tax generates now.

Peter Morici, a professor at Smith School of Business at the University of Maryland, penned an article[19] suggesting an 11% sales tax on everything. At least he was on the right track. Eleven percent of the $15 trillion economy would generate $1.65 trillion, about the same as the Fair Tax. Sadly, internet sniping with plenty of intellectually bankrupt thoughts from talking heads about the poor being abused and the rich getting richer will be rampant.

The present withholding system confiscates 7.65% of an employees' earnings and 15.3% of their self-employed person's earnings for the giant Ponzi scheme and Medi-scare. The income tax withheld is an amount based off a table or formula. Both are deducted from <u>gross</u> pay and are quoted as taxes on gross pay. The Fair Tax is doing the very same thing. Nobody says that if a person earns $500 this week and the government confiscates $38 for the giant Ponzi scheme/Medi-scare, and $50 for income tax that the tax rate is really 21% ($88 divided by $412 measured from the net) as opposed to 17% ($88 divided by $500, measured from the gross). If one were self-employed and setting aside $76 a week for their "contribution" to the Ponzi scheme plus the $50 for income tax, they would be left $374. Is their tax rate really 33% as opposed to 25%? I see arguing over the percentage as a distraction.

The REAL ISSUE is "what is the real cost of running the government"? Until all waste, fraud and corruption is out of government, social security is voluntary, we scale back the "American Empire" and a balance budget process is adopted we'll never know. I would propose that nothing less than 60% of the VOTING PUBLIC should permit an increase in the tax rate, though we should be aggressively looking to <u>reduce</u> the rate every year.

The research conducted by the Fair Tax movement also studied the effects of eliminating the income tax on prices of goods and services. Having been an accountant for thirty-five years I understand the costs of doing business and setting prices accordingly. I know firsthand that

---

[19] Peter Morici, The Street, July 2, 2013

all businesses have costs associated with operating under the present system. Those costs include record keeping so that you can file a tax return, paying an accountant to prepare a return that hopefully reduces one's chances of being terrorized, paying an overpriced accountant or tax attorney if you are attacked, (FYI all major corporations are audited every year) and if a business has a single employee it creates a whole series of report/forms, and the cost of matching their contribution to the giant Ponzi scheme. If you offer fringe benefits like health, welfare or retirement plans those require IRS filings as well. One's own income taxes and Ponzi scheme donation also has to be considered by small business owners when setting prices. The Fair Tax movement's research found these costs add 20-30% to the price of every good, service or product sold in this country. Eliminating the income tax would therefore allow prices to drop. While the naysayers will suggest vehemently that prices won't fall I have the utmost faith in American Free Enterprise (capitalism) that if businesses actually think they can add 23% to their price in the face of foreign competition and still get customers to buy it they're dead wrong.

Will prices actually drop be 20-30%? No one can be certain, however even half of that means your money goes farther and when the Fair Tax is added on you won't be paying any more than you would have with the income tax. As an example, let's assume you bought an article of clothing that now costs $10. After the fair tax is implemented the item should now sell for $8 using the low end of the assumption. When the Fair Tax is item would retail for $10.40. If prices were to drop 30% the new retail price would be $9.10.

The state sales tax would be computed on a lower amount (price minus the Fair Tax) so consumers would pay less in state sales taxes. That may not make a lot of governors happy but they have plenty of waste that needs cleaned up as well. The states can make up most of what they think they are going to lose when spending increases, which it will once the trillions locked up in overseas accounts and in retirement accounts flows back into our economy.

I've heard a national sales tax called a "utopian proposal" by conservatives and "most" (an unquantified term) voters don't seem to be sold on the idea. The idea that retailers (who now collect sales taxes in 45 states and DC) would be against it is intellectually dishonest as well as factually inaccurate. The idea also tends to get poo-poo-ed as a regressive tax falling heavier on the poor (those that vote for liberals and the robin-hood style government) than on rich people (you know the ones who create jobs). Just to set the record straight the federal gas tax (18.4 cents per gallon) is a regressive tax. The giant Ponzi scheme is a regressive tax. The "Medi-scare" tax is a regressive tax. The federal excise tax on airline tickets, jewelry, telephone bills and boats are regressive taxes. The federal/state tax on cigarettes and alcohol are regressive taxes. What about tolls on state or federal highways? I don't hear the MSNBC crowd jumping up and down about those taxes. Opponents of real tax reform especially a consumption tax are hypocrites. I don't see them pushing to abolish the sales tax in Florida, or NY, or California! If state governments can live with sales taxes as a major source of revenue why can't the feds? Florida and Texas have no individual income tax, have economies larger than many countries and people are flocking there. Ohio, where I grew up has seen a steady decline in its population over the past thirty years. The state income tax certainly hasn't drawn anybody there. When you add unions and weather to the mix it's easy to see why businesses and people leave.

The Fair Tax concept that was proposed over 15 years ago EXEMPTS used goods and services from the tax and gives the "poor" a check at the beginning of each month that presumes they will spend all their money on taxable items. They therefore could pay zero tax and still get a "pre-bate" check. How is that regressive? Or unfair? As prices come down by any amount triggered by the elimination of the income tax people can buy more goods and services. That's what stimulates the economy.

Considering most of the items bought and sold on the internet are "used" the whole notion of taxing the net should become moot. The giant box stores/retailers selling new merchandise on the net should collect the tax.

I guess you'd have to be a dirtbag, liar or power freak to understand liberal political logic. Only a dirtbag, liar and power freak would be unhappy that they could no longer have a tax system to spy on people's lives, play Robin Hood, demagogue success as evil, or retain over 90,000 trained terrorists. In this age of technology a national sales tax would not be an undue burden to the retailers or businesses. The federal government could collect money weekly if not daily and this nonsense about being able to pay its bills would be off the table. They'd have a continuous revenue stream.

During the 2012 presidential campaign former Governor Perry's "flat tax" was a non-starter for me and Michelle Bachman's bragging about being a federal tax attorney also was a real turnoff. At least the governor recognized that out of control government spending, asinine Federal Reserve policies and the devaluation of the dollar has forced a family of four to make $50,000 a year to stay above poverty. Even Herman Cain's 9-9-9 plan didn't go far enough or fast enough. Both plans wanted to pander to keeping middle class deductions that I already debunked.

Some Recent headlines and stories about the IRS from Yahoo News:

Corporate taxes: "Apple has allocated legally about 70 percent of its profits overseas, where tax rates are often MUCH lower than in the U.S. according to company filings".[20] Such tactics are part of "Perfectly Legal" by David Cay Johnson. The Fair Tax proponents believe corporations don't pay taxes, and don't care what the rates are, they just pass the tax on to consumers. Apple's profit $34.2 billion (2012) is only enough to run the government for three and half days even if they were taxed 100%. Apple paid $3.3 billion taxes worldwide but Treasury economist Martin A. Sullivan thinks they should have been $2.4 higher.

U.S. government workers owe $3.3 billion in delinquent taxes in 2013 according to a Reuters' story from May, 2014. "The number has not changed significantly since Sept. 30, 2011 when $3.5 billion was

---

[20]   NY Times/Associated Press, 2013 *Apple legally avoids billions in taxes*

delinquent." The IRS tried to sugar coat it by suggesting only 3.3% of the federal employees are delinquent as opposed to 8.7% of all taxpayers. If the IRS collected from their own they could keep the White House or national parks open for tourism rather shutting them down during fiscal crisis. Congress was voting on a bill in April, 2013 to make it impossible to work for the federal government if you have a large outstanding tax debt. What a concept, except rather than passing that law they should have been abolishing the income tax and balancing the budget.

IRS missing billions in ID Theft. (Josh Lederman, Associated Press, August 2, 2012) "The Internal Revenue Service may have delivered more than $5 billion in refund checks to identity thieves who filed fraudulent tax returns for 2011, Treasury Department investigators said Thursday. They estimate another $21 billion could make its way to ID thieves' pockets over the next five years."

IRS awards bonuses to 1,100 who owe back taxes, (Associated Press, Stephen Ohlemacher, April 22, 2014) "The Internal Revenue Service has paid more than $2.8 million in bonuses to employees with recent disciplinary problems including $1 million to workers who owe back taxes, a government investigator said Thursday"

Veterans Administration vs. the IRS. Debbie Burak of veteransaid.org writes (Feb, 2013) "I think the VA needs to take a crash course in how to do things from the IRS. These folks don't lose tax returns—they keep up with every dime you make. You can file on-line, they know if you haven't filed, and if you are owed a refund you can expect it in 30-45 days." (I filed a VA request for Aid and Assistance for my now deceased father in the spring of 2012. It NEVER got processed)

Tax fraud popular among prison inmates is the title of an ABC News article appearing on Yahoo! News on Jan. 17, 2013. "Tax fraud appears to be a popular pastime in the nation's prisons, but the Internal Revenue Service is catching on. The IRS detected more than 173,000 fraudulent tax returns from prison inmates last year, many of them using stolen identities and other false information in an attempt to get tax refunds".

24 IRS workers charged with theft. (Associated Press, Adrian Sainz, April 17, 2013) "Federal prosecutors say 24 current and former Internal Revenue Service employees have been charged with stealing government benefits". "….received more than $250,000 in benefits including unemployment insurance, food stamps, welfare and housing vouchers". Seems they are not all a bunch of choir boys. It's a shame stealing their paycheck isn't illegal as well.

Retired IRS Agent Who Investigated Brothel Boss Guilty of Prostitution Charges. (CBS News Las Vegas, Nov. 11, 2011) "A retired IRS agent who investigated a fugitive Nevada brothel boss and was partners in a failed rural Nevada bordello venture pleaded guilty Wednesday to transporting a California woman across state lines to commit prostitution" (Just a side note, the IRS seized/shutdown a brothel known as the Mustang Ranch in Nevada over ten years ago and tried to operate it and the even screwed that up.)

Judge rules against IRS in tax preparer suit. (Associated Press, Feb. 1, 2103) The judge rejected new regulations on tax preparers because the IRS had exceeded its authority.

Former Congressman Ron Paul has suggested there is no reason to license anything. It goes against "free" enterprise. When I was a young accountant looking for a job after getting my "CPA" license the gentleman interviewing me suggested that the fact that I had that license didn't mean I knew anything, just that I passed a test. The older I got the more I realized that applies to any license granted by any bureaucracy especially drivers' licenses.

If we can end the abusive income tax system and abolish the IRS it will send a message to every other federal agency that says "clean up your act or your next!" It would be the 21st century version of "the shot heard 'round the world" that started the America Revolution. Except we don't need to fire a single shot. We need a concerted technological driven movement to "clean out the swamp" at the ballot box by 2018. This country was a force that tore down the Berlin Wall and broke up the Soviet Union, it can abolish the income tax and the IRS.

To all future aspirants of federal office, tell the public the truth, have some courage of conviction and stop trying to work within a broken system. I believe the "silent majority" (the two thirds who didn't vote in 2014) is smarter than you think, are tired of liars and want real change. Congress's approval rating certainly can't go much lower, and America doesn't need another socialist in the White House, but there's always one waiting in the wings.

CHAPTER SIX

HOW DOES THE FAIR TAX APPLY TO ME??

So how's it going to work you may ask. We're going to turn out the lights on the IRS on December 31st in the year Congress enacts legislation, and start collecting the sales tax on January 1st of the new year. On January 2nd there will be a run on the moneys trapped in retirement accounts as people choose to pay off their mortgage, car loans, credit cards or buy a house, car, start a business or pay for their child's education. Talk about stimulus!

To explain how the Fair Tax relates to middle class families let's assume we have a husband and wife and two school age children making a combined income of $50,000 (which in my opinion is probably poverty). Right off the top the giant Ponzi Scheme/Medi-scare is confiscating $3,825. The income tax would be about $500. That's a total of $4,325 or about 8.75% of everything they made.

Under the Fair Tax this family would receive a "pre-bate" check of about $400/month and pay the Fair Tax when they purchase new goods and services. Existing mortgages, auto loans and credit card debts would not be subject to the Fair Tax, though food, gas, utilities, and insurance would be. Used items bought on-line, at garage sales, thrift stores and consignment shops etc. would not. Prices on everything they buy in the future will come down. All of which suggests this couple would have to spend 80% of their entire household income for goods and services the Fair Tax was applicable to use up the $4,325 they now pay in taxes plus the $4,800 in pre-bate checks. Obviously they wouldn't. As a bonus they never have to file an income tax return or deal with the IRS again. How is that a burden?

There are many celebrity supporters of the Fair Tax, including former Arkansas Gov. Mike Huckabee (R), former radio host Neal Boortz (author of two books on the subject), Sean Hannity, retired Georgia Senator Saxby Chambliss (R), former South Carolina Senator Jim Demint (R), former Oklahoma Senator Dr. Tom Osborn (R) and Herman Cain. Governor Romney ran as far away from the idea in his campaign as he could, even suggesting to the people of New Hampshire (who don't have a state sales tax) they didn't want a sales tax. It's no wonder he lost.

Mr. Boortz (now retired) claimed to have been a registered Libertarian in Florida but told his audience he was going to change his voting registration to "R" so that he could vote for Marco Rubio in his Senate primary contest (2010) against Charlie Christ, all because Mr. Rubio supported the Fair Tax. "Senator"/presidential candidate Rubio "jumped ship" now and claims to favor a flat tax.

Killing the income tax and "un-taxing" trillions in pension accounts, IRAs, 401Ks, annuities and overseas accounts will free up money that will come pouring into our economy and create millions of jobs. Foreign investment will be more attractive. Jobs create spending and spending creates more jobs. There may be inflation as millions of people will be looking to buy property and start businesses since a major impediment to making money in this country will be gone. But after a decade of sluggish growth it should be welcomed. Higher prices also mean higher revenues for the government. The people need to make certain politicians control the waste and re-evaluate the tax rate regularly. A constitutional amendment banning any income tax in the future should be passed.

Americans for Fair Taxation's research suggests 15% of the businesses in this country will collected 85% of the money under the Fair Tax. Even if the other 85% are "less than accurate" in their reporting they will pay tax when they spend the money. With so much "electronic money" now in the economy it would be just about impossible to be a 100% cash business and totally dishonest. If there is auditing to be done it can be done by the state sales tax people who would be losing tax dollars to cheaters as well. There should be serious financial penalties for failing to collect and transmit the tax. First time offenders should be hit with a penalty (for each offense) of 100% of the tax or $1,000 whichever is greater. A second offense should result in the revocation of the business license, a "front page story" glamorizing the fact and a hefty fine. Three strikes and you're outta here, but rather than a trip to Club Fed, real community service and a lifetime restitution plan and no government benefits.

The debate over how many paycheck stealing bureaucrats we need to carry over to "wind down" the old system will allow too much abuse to creep in. Once a consumption tax is passed the compliance factor with the old system will drop to near zero. I'm not sure that's a bad thing. The question is, do we waste more money trying to collect or persecute the now defunct income tax or do we just chalk it up to not being able to subsidize waste in the short run and do what Washington always does, PRINT MORE MONEY. Before we cry foul let's see how much the Fair Tax collects and get serious about waste.

Let's see what abolishing the IRS means:

   a) No more filings,
   b) No more audits,
   c) No more phony dependents,
   d) No more issues about employee vs. subcontractors,
   e) No more electronic fraud, identity theft
   f) An end to an entity never authorized by Congress,
   g) An end to corporate welfare,
   h) Business decisions made on sound economics.

    i)   No more class warfare/Robin Hood mentality,

    j)   No one to administer Obamacare,

    k) No more "tax crimes". We can eliminate judges, prosecutors, prisons, and ancillary pay check stealing bureaucrats,

    l)   We can cut the budget,

    m) No more TV ads about who's the best tax service. (How about using the same air time to expose waste?)

    n) No more wasted ink on the "10 common mistakes", "overlooked deductions", "abused deductions", and "reasons U get audited", and "what to in case of audit". All of the journalists can the write about government waste every day since it exists hourly.

    o) No more abusive tax-motivated transactions, shelters, overseas accounts (though asset protection may still be a concern) etc.. No living in fear.

    p) Drug dealers and anybody living in the underground economy will pay taxes.

    q) 90,000+ unemployed bureaucrats

That all sounds good to me, though it seems the IRS union is dead set against any reform that threatens their jobs-TO BAD.

Who gets the credit and class warfare should never be part of this discussion. It's good for all Americans. Who could be opposed to ridding us of a terrorist organization? 2013 was the 100th anniversary of the 16th amendment. As I asked in the prologue, why not try something else for 100 years? What are they afraid of? What are you afraid of? I'm betting within a decade our children and grandchildren will be asking "mom/dad--grandma/grandpa why did you let this go for so long?" For those that are part of the "Now Generation" ask yourself how long do you want to be a financial slave to a bunch of dirtbags, liars and power freaks? Rather than occupying Wall Street how about "Occupy IRS" and stay there until the system is abolished?

CHAPTER SEVEN

MY CASE

Friday October 13, 2006 was my "day that will live in infamy". That's the day I got a call from an IRS agent informing me I had been indicted by a grand jury and that I had to turn myself in the following Tuesday at 10 AM in Ocala, Florida. Even though the actual arraignment wasn't scheduled until 2 PM they wanted me early so they could screw with me.

I was placed in a holding cell for four hours and the temperature was deliberately cold. I had been warned about that. I was offered an extra shirt but it didn't help much. The cell had an adjoining lavatory but the toilet didn't have a seat on it. Glad I never had to use it. The fact that I hadn't shown up with an overpriced lawyer probably told them I couldn't afford one anyway and gave them latitude to screw with me. Knowing the system is rigged it would have been a waste of money anyway.

I was lying on an uncomfortable bench for most of the time and tried to catnap. Around lunchtime one of the marshals offered to get me lunch. What he offered and what came back were not even close, though I had already decided not to eat anything I couldn't swear wasn't tampered with. I left whatever it was, in the brown bag sitting on the bench when the arraignment hearing was finally called.

I was trying to figure out why I was in Ocala since I lived closer to Tampa, the grand jury sat in Jacksonville and the events they were investigating took place in Mount Dora. I never did get an explanation, though I chalked it up to "judge shopping" and the fact that my infamous co-defendant was Afro-American and the government didn't want to pick a jury in cities with large Afro-American populations (i.e. Tampa, Jacksonville or Orlando).

I was given an attorney (just to make the hanging look legal) who showed up about an hour before the actual hearing. When I asked him why my hearing had been delayed and he told me some "Hollywood actor was being arraigned". I suggested he should stick his nose in the courtroom because maybe it had something to do with my case. Obviously it did and he knew it. However, there was NO "Hollywood Actor" being arraigned because Wesley Snipes (the actor in question) wasn't even in the country let alone the state of Florida. Either this attorney didn't know the truth, wasn't told the truth or lied to me.

I was charged with filing a false claim and conspiracy to defraud the government. The penalty could have been probation to 10 years in a federal prison. (The charges never merited more than probation because there was NO victim and NO damages). The lawyer entered a not guilty plea and I was released on my own recognizance, with the stipulation that I try to stay employed. That didn't last long because the company I was working for let me go three weeks later claiming the publicity might spill over into the media camping out in their parking lot and a fear of an attack by the IRS.

With all the normal legal wranglings, motions and maneuvering and a change of lawyers by Mr. Snipes, the case didn't even come to trial until 15 months later. During that time I had one meeting with my court appointed attorney that lasted less than 2 hours, yet I spent 3 hours one-way driving to his office. He claimed the distance was why we didn't meet more often, as though that should hinder a search for the truth and a proper defense. He did suggest that he thought I wasn't guilty (which I knew anyway) because the definition of conspiracy "…by craft, trickery and deceit" wasn't met here. I was adamant about the fact that I wasn't pleading guilty to something that had no victims, no damages and was a free speech issue at heart.

It's my position that the only "conspiracy" that ever existed was one of trying to get to the truth and the IRS attempting to suppress it. But when the government is wrong they ATTACK, not respect due process. EVERY return being challenged by the government had a statement attached asking for due process (copy below). Maybe the IRS didn't owe me due process, but they did owe every single taxpayer. If taxpayers weren't entitled to due process (a hearing under the Administrative Procedures Act) what was the basis for that denial? The truth hurts.

ATTACHMENT TO FORM 1040/1040X:

NAME:

SOCIAL SECURITY NUMBER:

This return is being filed on the basis of the IRS regulation 26CFR 1.861-8 which identifies all of the TAXABLE sources of income within the United States of America. As far as I have been able to determine, none of the receipts of this taxpayer(s) came from any of these sources.

Since, according to 1.861-8(4), the TAXABLE source must FIRST be determined before taxable income can be determined, these receipts must therefore be exempt from taxation. The calculations on the attached 1040 (1040X) form reflect that position. Based on those calculations, there should be a complete refund of all moneys paid in.

"(T)he purpose of the rule that federal agencies are required to abide by their own regulations even where such regulations are more generous than required by law is to prevent unjust discrimination and denial of adequate notice of procdures by the agency in violation of due proess."

United States v. Newell, 578 F.2nd 827,828 (9th Cir. 1978)

For federal tax purposes, federal regulations govern.

Dodd v. U>S., D.C.N.J. 1963, 223 F.Supp. 785, affirmed 345 F.2d 715

Should the IRS disagree with this position, please schedule an Administrative Law Judge Review on this matter pursuant to the Administrative Procedures Act 5 USC 556(d).

The IRS, under the Freedom of Information Act, has admitted that it is subject to the Administrative Procedures Act. That being the case the courts have ruled, in numerous cases, that we would be entitled to a "fair trial" admnstratively. Some of those rulings are listed below.

"Due process in administrative hearings includes a fair trial conducted in accordance with fundamental principles of fair play and applicable procedural standards established by law, and administrative convenience or necessity cannot override this requirement."

Russel-Newman Mfg. Co. v. N.L.R. B.
C.A. Tex 1966, 370 F2d 980

"Under the Administrative Procedure Act, the proponent of a rule or order has the burden of proof. Burden of proof means "going forward with the evidence".

Bosma v U.S. Dept. of Agriculture, C.A. 9, 1984, 754 F2nd 804

Other cites: Ideal Farm, Inc. v Benson, D.C. N.J. 1960, 181 F Supp 62
affirmed 288 F2d 608, Certiorari denied 83 Sct 1087
327 US 965, 10 Led2d 128

: U.S. v Brad, D.C Cal 1968

: Amos Treat and Co v Securities and Exchange Commission
306 F2d 260 (1962), 113 US App D.C. 100

In June of 2001 the IRS had to hire a public relations firm to deal with the issue that became the heart of my case. A memo they released was so legally unsound that no one signed it. It was not issued on any stationery of any governmental agency, yet the IRS tried to bluff the taxpayers by attaching it to the responses they sent out when rejecting a refund claim. No official title (or authority) of the author was listed. What was cited as "case law" were a bunch of NON-binding Tax Court cases and two off-point Supreme Court cases.

Prior to either case being filed one of Eddie Kahn's clients/taxpayer, when questioning why their claim had been rejected, got a letter from the Cincinnati Service Center. The letter was mechanically signed with the surname of Arlinghaus-Clem. It was such a unique name that I always remembered it. While I hope the person was real, there was no badge number associated with the name. Having learned of the IRS's proclivity for using aliases it made me wonder. The letter said "...the courts have rejected...." these types of claims. Sadly the name of those courts, the case cite, or the jurisdiction was not part of the letter. A follow up letter asking for that information went unanswered. If the IRS's position was on such solid ground why couldn't they provide their alleged proof? The fact was, there was no Supreme Court case on the issue.

This was just one of many hundreds of letters my clients/taxpayers received over the years that were/are typical of government agencies and politicians. While they put words on a piece of paper and can technically get away with claiming they "responded", their "response" is very seldom respons-IVE. They are incapable of giving an "on-point" answer, and deathly afraid of taking a position, never-mind putting it in writing.

Prior to the criminal persecution I was attacked in a civil action (2002) seeking an injunction that basically spit on a taxpayer's right to due process, free speech, to say nothing of a search for the truth. The subsequent visit by the criminal investigators allowed me to assert my fifth-amendment rights in the civil case and delay that case. It didn't make the judge in the case happy and three years later she simply issued a ruling that closed the case. I discussed the issues at the heart of case with three separate attorneys, two of which claimed to be "tax attorneys". One of them told me point blank I didn't do anything wrong. The statements and explanations that were a part of the filings told the IRS exactly what was being done, why it was being done, and what remedy (due process) the taxpayer(s) expected and were entitled to. NONE of it constituted "craft, trickery and deceit". As one lawyer suggested, ".. you hit 'em right between the eyes…" and didn't do anything criminal.

The other attorney I spoke with could not dispute the facts I presented but said "good luck finding a federal judge who will stand up for it". So much for the concept of truth, justice and the American way. All of the attorneys I spoke with after the criminal indictment told me that when the government goes to trial they win 90+% of the time. One of Mr. Snipes' attorneys put the number at a percentage closer to body temperature. After watching how you can rig a jury, threaten witnesses, suppress evidence and give the persecutors a "mulligan" if they botch their case, how could they lose? I had no delusions of winning but the sentence I was given was excessive. I can't imagine any attorney working in such a corrupt system. I wonder how many people would drop a quarter into a slot machine that had a sign on it that said, "Good Luck, we win 98.6% of the time". Do you think they'd be screaming "FIX" or "RIGGED"? Or complaining to the regulators?

In 2006 before the indictment, I was subpoenaed to provide a handwriting sample. My signature must have been on thousands of tax returns over 35 years so comparing them would have been very easy. Since the "Turn America into a Police State Act" was now law they could have gotten a copy of my signature from any of the banks I had accounts in and from the checks I wrote. But that would be intelligent behavior. That wasn't bad enough but they wanted me to go all the way to Jacksonville to give them the handwriting sample. Jacksonville was where the grand jury had been convened but was a 5 hour drive one way (north) for me. The agent who was dogging me was based in Fort Myers (70 miles away south). The government also has offices in Tampa, Orlando, Maitland and Ocala that

I could have gone to but again that would have been intelligent behavior. The real "icing on the cake" was that they reimbursed be for my travel (over $300) to offer evidence against myself. When I got the check I took it to the bank and handed it to the lady at the drive thru window to deposit. The lady told me the check was dated two months in the future. Obviously I never looked at the date and had no reason to think the check wasn't good. I sent the check back and wait for another one, which I got with a lame apology. To further suggest this was government idiocy at its finest, during the trial the prosecution felt it necessary to call a handwriting expert (more $$$ wasted) to prove I signed the return in question. My lawyer and I stipulated to that.

After the arraignment I spoke with my court appointed lawyer on the phone on two other occasions. All of which hardly qualified as a preparation for a proper defense. There was never any settlement offer or plea deal made that I was aware of. I remember giving the attorney the names of a handful of people who could be possible witnesses or could educate him on the issues at the heart of the case but I have no idea if he ever contacted them since he never called any witnesses at the trial.

One of those possible witnesses was a former IRS agent who was holding a seminar in Sarasota, Florida in January of 2007 that I made a point to attend. I wanted to talk about my case and their being a witness. This person told me that legal counsel had advised against any such involvement. I found out that the IRS made a habit of threatening anybody who could be a witness in any case they thought was a "tax protestor case".

A former Federal Court of Appeals Judge Edith Jones, suggested in a speech in February, 2003 before the Federalist Society of the Harvard Law School that the system was "corrupted almost beyond recognition." I submit to you that it hasn't gotten any better in the later years.

I was amazed that even though Mr. Snipes is Afro-American there was not one such person among the <u>prospective</u> jurors being interviewed, obviously not on the jury or maybe in the jury pool. I guess walking upright and breathing may be the only criteria that make any group a "jury of your peers". A blind person could see that wasn't a jury of his peers but the judge rejected his lawyers' objection.

In my case I'm a Caucasian male, a college graduate, retired accountant, Roman Catholic, Italian ancestry, registered independent and straight. I don't think anybody on the jury fit that profile, so what is "a jury of your peers"? I have never served on a jury and avoided it any time I was contacted. I'm sure they wouldn't want me anyway. My first encounter with cops just before the Miranda decision came out left a lasting bad taste in my mouth for all of them, though I do not condone violence aimed at them. Corruption in the legal system, the phony "war on drugs", and the whole illegal immigrant issue hasn't made me a fan of politicians, lawyers or judges either.

It was quite obvious to me during the jury selection process (that took 3 days) no one who could think for themselves or question the government was going to be on this jury. A woman I only remember as a "pistol-packin' grandma" was interviewed but rather quickly dismissed when she told the judge she owned a gun, knew how to use it and scared off an intruder after being asked by the judge if anybody had been the "victim" of a crime.

When the trial finally got underway the defense team had to present a list of potential witnesses that the jurors may know or have some contact with. The list included Muhammad Ali, Tom Brokaw, the IRS Commissioner, former IRS agent Joe Bannister and a handful of other high profile names, NONE of whom were ever called to testify. I remember telling one of Mr. Snipes' attorneys that I'd love to see him put the IRS Commissioner on the stand but knew it would never happen.

Almost from the start the third defendant, Eddie Kahn, refused to take part in the proceedings. He had asked to have "advice of counsel" but wanted to represent himself. The judge appointed him an attorney but

Mr. Kahn rejected his help and spent the rest of the trial in his cell at the county jail. (I wasn't impressed with the attorney they tried to give him) Mr. Kahn challenged the judge as not being an Article III judge, but the judge did produce the proof that Mr. Kahn asked for. I was majorly disappointed in Mr. Kahn because he now had a stage upon which to confront the IRS about all the issues he had been running around the country expounding, yet chose not to. I believe Mr. Snipes' defense team thought he would hurt their case by exploring "tax protester arguments" and asked him not to participate.

Mr. Kahn had moved to Panama a few years earlier thinking there was no extradition treaty with Panama, which may have been true but the U.S. government talked Panamanian officials in declaring him "persona non-grata" and had him deported into the waiting arms of the U.S. Marshals. Subsequently Panama, with U.S. support, was given one of the rotating seats on the UN Security Council. Coincidence? I doubt it.

Throughout the trial information that was supposed to be given to the defense as part of the discovery process, known as "Jenks" material, was handed over by the prosecutors, but not until 5:00 on the day before it would be relevant. That meant that the defense had to probably go without sleep or less sleep to evaluate the material. What happened to professional courtesy? Or honor among thieves?

The prosecution case took about two weeks and then they rested. Immediately Mr. Snipes' team also rested, and my attorney chimed in as well. I was stunned. I thought now it's the good guys turn to present a case and they "rested"! I was hoping for a "kick-ass" defense and got nada. During the lunch break I confronted the lead attorney for Mr. Snipes and said, "what the #&#%^E are you doing?" Rather than a defense, what I got was a real education about the federal court system. It seems after the government's attorneys present what's called its "case in chief" the defense gets a turn to present its case. After possibly destroying the prosecutions' case (and watching thousands of taxpayer dollars go down the drain) the court gives the prosecution a mulligan, a do-over, an "oopsy" affectionately called a "rebuttal case". (The government certainly wants to make sure they get a conviction). Mr. Snipes' defense team didn't want to give the government that opportunity. Their thinking was that the case was held in the wrong jurisdiction (to hell with the facts and issues) and they could win in closing arguments.

In my only conversation, prior to the trial, with Mr. Snipers in 2001 he assured me he was a Florida resident when I was following up on a tax notice he'd received from the state of Florida regarding its intangible tax.

I think my attorney was not willing to waste too much "legal capital" defending some alleged tax protestor since a large share of his income came from court appointed cases. I thought both his opening and closing statements were fair at best and told him so after his closing. He told me he had been doing this for fifteen years and I told him if he did another fifteen he might get it right. This was always a free speech/due process issue and he never took an aggressive position towards either.

There was no evidence presented that would support the alleged "false claim" filed against Mr. Snipes' in any way contained false information. He was a real person. The social security number was his. The statistical data was correct, and the issue in question was documented and attached as required. While the IRS may not have liked the issues raised or agreed with them, that doesn't destroy a person's right to make them. There was no U.S. Supreme Court decision on the matter. The IRS could have simply rejected ANY claim in question and LET DUE PROCESS PLAY OUT. Unfortunately that could have opened the door to Mr. Snipes' filing a civil action in U.S. District Court (which then makes it a very public issue) rather than handling it in the phony "Tax Court". Mr. Snipes could have demanded a jury trial and presented his case. (Which the government would never have allowed. They don't believe in the 6th Amendment either.) He had the resources to do so. There is no doubt in my mind he would have lost that case on some convoluted decision. But the issues raised would come before the public, IRS witnesses would have been cross-examined and any decision that wasn't on point, legally sound and backed up by case law would have smelled funny in the eyes of the public and exposed the system for what it is – corrupt.

There is also the issue of "independence" in such cases. How can someone whose next paycheck and government pension (which come from the Treasury Department) be truly "financially independent" when ruling in a case involving the U.S. Treasury? In the private sector such financial entanglements are grounds for auditors to disqualify themselves in rendering an opinion as to the fair presentation of an entity's financial statements. But more to the point there would never have been a basis for a criminal persecution, which is what the government does when it's wrong. They ATTACK.

In 2001 "We the People" a privately funded tax honesty organization placed four full page ads, questioning many aspects of the Tax Code, in the *USA Today*. The Senate Finance Committee did not appreciate the ads and called (then) Commissioner Rossotti to inquire what the IRS was doing about it. The management of the paper was told to stop taking money from We the People and running future ads. NEVER, did the IRS demand equal space or the opportunity to place their own ad that clearly and legally refuted anything that was said. Four other citizen/taxpayers who were members of We the People were also attacked individually by the IRS over positions they had taken and were demanding answers. So much for "free speech", "freedom of the press" and the first amendment "right to redress grievances".

The prosecution also chose to glamorize the fact that the word "no" had been inserted into the statement a taxpayer signs saying they are signing their tax return under penalty of perjury, on the return filed by Mr. Snipes. There was no evidence submitted as to how such a modification could have been made or who made it. The truth is I didn't actually prepare the return in question. It was done by someone who was associated with Mr. Kahn's organization prior to my involvement. I found it in a file they had on Mr. Snipes. I reviewed it, attached the supporting documents and accepted responsibility for it. I never had any reason to look at the "fine print" or to suspect it could be altered. This point seems to be the entire basis for the whole "false claim" charge. If in fact altering this statement was such a heinous act, the return should have been rejected as defective. Mr. Snipes, or any taxpayer, should have the opportunity within the statute of limitation to correct any "defects" in the claim and re-file it. If the return was defective, how can there be a bona fide claim, fraudulent or otherwise? That issue should have been the focal point of my attorney's summation.

After the defense rested the judge commented that this had been a well-argued case. I thought to myself what "arguments?" The defense folded. In his instructions to the jury the judge simply said the issue in question was "without merit" but didn't explain it. On Friday February 1, 2008, the third day of deliberations, the jury reached a verdict. Eddie Kahn and I were both found guilty of conspiracy and filing a false claim. Wesley was found not guilty on both of those charges and in a totally amazing verdict, guilty of failing to file tax returns for 3 of the six years he was charged with and not guilty on three others. (In July of 2010 one of Mr. Snipes' attorneys said he received an unsolicited e-mail from one of the jurors. The e-mail said "there were 3 on the jury that felt this way and told us he was guilty before they even heard/seen the first piece of evidence/testimony...") What's up with that? How could I be guilty of filing a false claim? Both Mr. Snipes and my signature were on the return. There was no evidence that he was coerced. So what constitutes "filing"?

In May of 2010 money manager Kenneth I. Starr, Mr. Snipes' former accountant and a witness for the government, was charged in a criminal complaint that he defrauded his celebrity and socialite clients of at least $59 million. Mr. Starr was under investigation at the time of the trial. He eventually went to prison.

The sentence (54 months) I got for a victimless, damage-less situation was excessive. If the IRS or Treasury Department incurred (or would have incurred) any "damages" they would have been self-inflicted. They have/had the power, authority and wherewithal to reject any return/

claim they choose. In fact testimony brought out the fact they have what they call "a funny box" where returns that don't meet their standards are singled out. The fact that they made refunds to taxpayers making the same claim can only be attributed to bureaucratic inefficiency. That doesn't make me guilty, yet they spit on my and every taxpayer's right to due process and free speech. Sameena vs. Air Force (9th Circuit, 1998) and Near vs. Minnesota (Supreme Court, 1923) are two cases that support my position.

The sentencing hearing was another circus. Mr. Snipes had a whole new team of overpriced lawyers that suggested to him that paying the government money would minimize his sentence. A blind man could also see that wasn't going to happen, though it should have. The dumbest thing he did was give the IRS $5,000,000. The worst case scenario had him going to prison for 3 years without giving them a penny. He took bad advice, wasted money on a new legal team, spent $5 million and still got a 3 year sentence. The whole objective here was to show "we're tough on crime" (except when you grossly mismanage public money, rig a jury, suppress evidence, don't prosecute 11 million law breakers) and nobody is above the law (except for politicians and bureaucrats). His attorneys paraded a handful of celebrity witnesses in hopes of getting a light sentence. It didn't do any good. The lead prosecutor asked one celebrity judge "do you pay your taxes?" Which was totally irrelevant! The charge was "failure to file" not "failure to pay" (which is not a crime).

The thing I found especially amusing is that both the judge and the prosecutor refused to take the $5 million dollar check, claiming they are not collection agents of the IRS. After the lunch break one of the IRS people sitting in the gallery raised his hand and said "I'll take that check". What a waste of money. (His attorney claimed it was $6.5 million during his 11th hour interview with Larry King that I watched.) Not only did he waste $5 million he should have reported to prison and would have been out two years sooner and saved all the money he spent on filing an appeal that had a 95% chance of being rejected. I was told the government has to let a few cases go in favor of the appellant in order to give credibility to the whole appeals process and the bureaucrats it employs. I think it's a waste of money. His attorneys should have fought for the one year halfway house/home confinement time the newly signed 2nd Chance Act provided and their client could have been "out" in 18 months.

My court appointed attorney knew filing an appeal was a waste of time and so he never filed one. He also had no clue as to where I might be sent or any understanding of the various security levels used by the prison system. While judges can recommend a particular prison, the Bureau of Prisons does what it wants and has a real attitude about being told how to do their job. They feel the inmates are all "property" and they can do what they want, if they want and when they want with complete immunity.

In 2009 I wrote to my court appointed lawyer and asked him to file a motion with the court and petition the judge modify my sentence to guarantee me the benefits of the "The Second Chance Act". That bill had been signed into law about a week before the sentencing hearing and made me eligible for up to a year of halfway house time and home confinement. The lawyer wrote back and said his time for representing me had expired and to take the issue up with the prison personnel. The prison personnel simply followed the orders of former BOP Director Harley Lappin who thumbed his nose at the law.

In December of 2009 the attorney called the prison camp I was assigned to and arranged a "legal call" with me. When my counselor told me of it I was surprised since the attorney had previously blown me off. Curious, I took the call. Allegedly Mr. Snipes needed an attorney with a Florida license for his appeals team and not knowing anybody else they asked mine if he was interested. The purpose of his call to me was to ask if I would sign off on any possible "conflict of interest" claim and allow him to make some Christmas money. "Mama needs Christmas money" was his comment. I told him if he did for Mr. Snipes what he did for me Mr. Snipes might never get out. He then told me what a wonderful job he had done. He was going to send me a paper to sign, though it never came. All of the "jailhouse" lawyers I discussed it with said, NO WAY. But the ultimate decision maker was my wife. She said "(expletive deleted) him", he hung up on me when I called to ask a question". He certainly deserved a lump of coal that Christmas. I never did get any paper.

In December of 2010 I clipped two items from a copy of Hip Hop magazine was passing around the camp, they were both about Mr. Snipes and the case. The first articles states:

> Declaring taxes unfair and that the IRS did not have the authority to collect them, in 2006 the blade star decided that he didn't want to pay them anymore. He became a fugitive of justice, held up in Nigeria for months where he was shooting a film. Upon his return to the states, Snipes was arrested and charged with federal tax-fraud and conspiracy charges, owing the government more than $2.7 million in back taxes. He could have faced up to 16 years in prison, but a judge found him not guilty, though he was convicted on three misdemeanor counts of failing to file a tax return.

The erroneous statements in this short article are amazing and young people read this and run with it. First, Mr. Snipes was charged with failure to file going back to 1999. An indictment came down in 2006. The word fugitive implies you have been charged and are wanted and your whereabouts unknown. None of that was true. I believe Mr. Snipes was filming was in Namibia, Africa. There were no "federal tax fraud" charges. There was a filing a false claim charge. The amount of money was over $2.7 million. His lawyers offered $5 million the day of the sentencing and a subsequent article in Hip Hop put the amount at $15 million. The judge didn't find anything, a jury found him not guilty on some charges and guilty on others. The camp he went to allegedly had 2 man rooms and only 300 inmates.

It's a real shame the truth (or the facts) has no place in what is loosely called journalism today. One print media story called me "a renowned outlaw tax evader."

Part Two
DOJ/BOP

CHAPTER ONE

"CLUB FED"

I received a "designation" letter on June 20, 2008 and was given 10 days to report to the federal prison camp at Pensacola, Florida (affectionately known herein as Club Fed). It is a minimum security facility and is considered a "work camp" because the inmates are farmed out to the Navy to maintain the grounds at the Naval Air Station in Pensacola, a golf course at Whiting Field, a Unicor operation and the grounds at the Air Force base in Eglin.

Once I surrendered myself to the Bureau of Prisons to begin my sentence, over the next three and a half years I got an up close and personal look at more waste, fraud, abuse and government idiocy all in an effort to show "we're tough on crime". I came to I believe there is a special place in hell for those running the Bureau of Prisons and its individual facilities.

Right after checking in I was escorted to the admission/discharge area commonly called R & D. There I was told to strip. My clothes were confiscated and sent back to my wife. I had the usual body cavity search all the time wondering what kind of person gets off doing body cavity searches. I was given the traditional orange jump suit that screamed "newbie" and escorted to the medical department.

Medical

The lady I was handed off to was a para-medic and she told me I had to have a TB test. Questioning that, I was told that men from various parts of the US and Puerto Rico were sent here and the BOP couldn't always be sure if they had been properly treated for TB. I thought this country wiped out TB over sixty years ago, but it was a "hot button" at this place. I never had a TB test in the real world, but here we all had to have one every year. It's a shame they weren't as concerned about high cholesterol, gout, arthritis, and cancer as they were about TB.

After the TB test I got to meet the doctor/clinical director. He wanted to know what medication I was on and a bit of my health history. I was on three prescriptions at the time that were prescribed by a doctor in the outside world. I say that because subsequent research by my family revealed this person was not licensed to practice (or dispense) medicine anywhere in the United States or the state of Florida. After only a few minutes talking with him I knew he was a quack and just a paycheck-stealing government contractor/employee.

Two of the meds I was taking, a statin and time release niacin, were for elevated cholesterol and both were keeping mine under control. The statin is a $4/month drug and the niacin had just gone over the counter and cost about $7 for a 90 day supply. The other script was an anxiety drug and also cost $4/month. The "doctor" actually called my wife while she was on her way back home and told her to get my regular doctor to write a letter explaining why he had prescribed these meds and what they were for. He told my wife "we're going to take real good care of him". What a lie that was. The doctor did give me a six month script to get the statin from the prison pharmacy but cancelled the other two pills. My outside doctor didn't honor a request from my wife citing privacy issues, so I had to write to him and make the request myself. He never responded to me or the prison "doctor".

Over the next three and a half years the doctor and I played a game of "on again off again" with my cholesterol medication. Every time it was time to renew my script they had to draw blood (waste money). Every test suggested my cholesterol level was in "acceptable" range and so the quack stopped the medication. Three or four months later when I had another blood test my cholesterol level was elevated. A first year med student could figure that one out. One of the first times I went in to get my results I spoke with the physician's assistant (PA) that I was assigned. He had "consummate bureaucrat" written all over him and actually had a sign on his door counting down the days until his "sentence" (i.e. retirement) was over. He bragged about never having lost a patient in 19 years. When I asked who was caring for Mr. Vega, a diabetic who dropped dead in the room I was assigned to just before I got there, he went silent. Camp scuttlebutt suggested nobody ever died at the camp they all died in the ambulance on the way to the hospital.

This rocket scientist suggested I needed to change my diet. Let's see, I'm trapped in a situation where you eat what they put in front of you or starve and he says I have to change my diet. His specific advice was to take the skin off the chicken. I always took the skin off my chicken from the time I was 6 years old. (as a point of reference what the kitchen called chicken was probably pigeon, it was so small) Then the quack got into the conversation and suggested the fact that my mother (who was 80 at the time) was still alive (even though she had bypass surgery at 62 and a stent at 72) meant I didn't have "a family history" of heart disease. My mother was fortunate to have very capable doctors and obviously insurance and Medicare to pay for her treatment. The prison system suggests you have "free" medical care, but remember when one pays nothing they often get nothing. What this facility passed off as medical care was tantamount to attempted murder. Five inmates besides Mr. Vega died while I was a guest at "Club Fed". Two of them, Mike Dooley and David Whitfield, were guys I knew. Mike was my first bunkmate. The first day or so that I was there he told me that if I had a problem with anyone to let him know. Thankfully I never had to.

Mike was a smoker and chewed tobacco and had a family history of cancer so he was probably playing Russian roulette by even touching tobacco products. He had a problem with his back in January of 2009 after playing basketball, but the quack never ordered the proper test (an MRI) to diagnose his problem. By the time an MRI was ordered (July '09) Mike was so full of cancer they stopped the test. He was transferred to a medical facility in the prison system in North Carolina. He died 3 months later and was only 44. His family had tried to get him a compassionate release but the wheels of bureaucracy moved to slow. From what I read recently the whole compassionate release concept authorized by Congress is wantonly ignored by the BOP. They must be afraid the inmate may be the recipient of a divine miracle and would somehow escape the full punishment of the law. It's just another example of lack of accountability over paycheck stealing bureaucrats and government idiocy.

David died in transit to Tampa to attend a hearing that was probably going to result in a sentence reduction. He died from complications related to a hemorrhoid procedure performed by the quack before he left Pensacola. He actually didn't feel well enough to make the trip and wanted to postpone it, but the BOP sent him anyway. If what happened to these two was not malpractice I don't know what is. Negligence doesn't even come close.

One of the first things I found out after settling in, was that inmates couldn't get sick on Wednesday. There is no "sick call" on that day or Saturday or Sunday. The universal treatment was generic Tylenol and drink lots of water.

Though I never had a flu shot before I came to "Club Fed" I was now rethinking that. I was concerned about the effectiveness of what vaccine the prison was actually being given and if I had a reaction to it I'd probably be dead before they treated me. I decided against having one, and never did. I stopped in the chapel every morning and thanked God for keeping me in good health. One of the guys on my work detail in 2009 who was a real germ-a-phobe caught the flu anyway and spent a couple days in quarantine. He blamed it on one of the other guys he rode with to and from their work area. The other guy also caught the flu and ended up in the quarantine room.

I had my wife contact a personal injury/wrongful death law firm and ask them what to do in case she ever needed them. They basically told her to have me document every time I sneezed and had contact with the medical department, demand written responses, keep a log and to send copies of everything to her. Sadly, anybody that doesn't have an advocate on the outside of a prison is truly at the mercy of whatever person is assigned their care. From what I gathered talking with guys who had been in other prisons the health care was pretty much the same all over. It sucked.

My experiences with the medical department over three and a half years included:

a) A seven week wait to get new glasses after I broke mine at Christmas time of 2008. Being nearsighted I should have refused to work or handle any tools or equipment until I got glasses. My wife took my old prescription to Wal-Mart and had a new pair of glasses made. Wal-Mart agreed to mail them for my wife, but when the package got to the camp it was rejected because they didn't have the required authorization label, stamp, form, or whatever. My wife was livid since she had called and asked if she could send the new glasses. You would think these people could have x-rayed the box, opened the box, inspected the glasses, tested the glasses, or done anything that satisfied them the glasses weren't dangerous and gotten them to me. Instead I had to go beg a form from my "counselor", send it to my wife and she had to resend the glasses. A fine example of bureaucratic idiocy. Luckily a couple of guys on my work detail found an epoxy that mended my broken glasses temporarily.

b) An 11 month wait for a simple dental exam. I had a tooth that fell apart and I wanted to see what the dentist might do. When I finally got the appointment I refused to let them do anything and had to sign a bunch of forms stating as much. Two years later they had me on a list for a dental appointment claiming I had made such a request. When I assured them I wouldn't do such a thing they did say the request was old. Government inefficiency strikes again. I had to sign another statement that I was "refusing" treatment.

c) Inmates over 60 were "entitled" to an annual physical. Younger ones every two years. Unfortunately you have to beg for the physical. There is no automatic scheduling like there is for their silly TB tests, flu shots or teeth cleaning. I made a request for a physical in late 2009 and it took a year before all of the proper tests were completed. I was now eligible for ANOTHER physical but said, what's the use? A prime example of the government deliberately trying to discourage inmates from asking for help.

d) I asked for X-rays of both wrists as part of my physical because I had sharp pains in them while twisting or rotating them. I suspected arthritis. I was sent to a local hospital as an outpatient for the X-rays a few days later. I was given the results for one wrist but not the other one. It did show some arthritis but no treatment was recommended and no restrictions on what kind of work I should avoid were considered.

e) I developed an infection in my right arm that probably was some type of staph infection. The female PA who was on duty when I went in did get me the proper antibiotics with an injection three days in a row that cleared up the problem. Even though I was recovering the quack still wanted to inspect my arm, for all the good that did.

f) My wife got tired of the on again, off again tactics with my cholesterol meds and wrote to Senator Bill Nelson's (D-Fla) office. His office contacted the BOP on my behalf but I actually had gotten the pills refilled a few days earlier. They weren't real happy about a contact from a US Senator. Remember these are pills that cost $4/month or $48/year. My family would have gladly paid for them, but nobody tells the BOP what to do, and there is no accountability.

g) As part of the one physical I did request, I asked to have a colonoscopy. The quack wanted to know why I wanted a colonoscopy. I told him because I was 62 and never had one (and I wanted to spend some of the BOP's money). After some weeping and gnashing of teeth they scheduled one for me at a local hospital. The test was scheduled for a Monday in November of 2010. On the Friday beforehand my wife called the camp and wanted to know where the test was going to be done and who the doctor would be. The next morning I got paged to come to the medical department. The male nurse who was on duty chastised me for telling my wife about the test and that it somehow constituted a security breach. It seems long, long ago in a place far, far away some woman went to hospital to do bodily harm to her inmate husband so she could collect his insurance money. Allegedly innocent bystanders were harmed, so using the "one size fits all" mentality family members were not supposed to know about off premises inmate medical procedures.

The male nurse who told me all this, threatened to cancel the test. I said "go ahead", I wasn't going to keep my family in the dark and reminded him of the guys who died while stuck there. I'm sure the fact that I gave up on the test made them think their idiot mentality was right. My wife wasn't too happy when I told her she was a potential security risk.

h) In late April of 2011 while working at my job at the recycling plant on the naval base I stepped on a manhole cover trying to move something in the way of the forklift operator. The cover gave way and I fell into the manhole. It happened so suddenly it shocked me. I was only a couple feet deep but I hit my left side on the edge of the iron collar and was afraid I had seriously cut myself. Luckily there was no blood or wounds but I was sore. I reported the fall to my supervisor, filled out a bunch of forms and he reported it to the camp. Nobody came to get me to have me checked out. I spent most of remainder of the day lying down. When the shift ended and my detail got back to the camp I limped to the medical department. I was told that the doctor was too busy to see me and I'd have to comeback in the morning. The fact that I fell didn't mean a thing. At a minimum I knew I needed an X-ray. My side was very painful and it was uncomfortable for me to crawl up and down the ladder of my bunk and trying to sleep that night. The next day I decided to skip medical because they wouldn't do anything before Monday or Tuesday and I went to work. I'd rather be away from the camp.

My supervisor wouldn't make me do anything I couldn't do and if it became obvious I couldn't work they would again call the camp. Hopefully someone would have the good sense to come and get me and see that I got attention. On Monday I went to the medical department and finally got to see the quack. When he asked why I wanted an X-ray I lifted my shirt and showed him the rather large black and blue bruise in my kidney area. He ordered an X-ray but it didn't happen until Friday which was now a week since I fell. Thank God I was slowly feeling better. I never actually saw the X-rays but allegedly there were no fractures. In March of 2012, while on home confinement, I went to see a real doctor and have a real physical. That doctor ordered a bone scan after I voiced my concerns about arthritis. The bone scan revealed that what I was originally told wasn't true and X-rays are not conclusive in such matters. I actually had two cracked ribs on my left side and one on my right that were healed. I was assured only bone scans (a test that you don't order when you're worried about the budget) will give you accurate results.

Those are just my horror stories with the medical department. My best friend Don, Bob U., Ted G., Mr. C. and Tom N. are more examples of neglect. One inmate, Jim C. spent 13 days in the hospital for staph infection. They had no choice but to send him. He told me his hospital bill was over $200,000. I'd bet that pretty much busted the camp's medical budget for the year.

Nobody at this camp received the death penalty or was doing life without parole so it's my position that if you want to send them here and run a slave labor camp you'd better take care of their medical needs. Yes there were a handful of inmates who were daily visitors to the medical department complaining about the least little thing and hoping to get out of work, but sending people to work who aren't fit is arrogant. If this is what "government run health care" is like God help us all now that we have Obamacare.

My Room.

After my initial visit with the medical department I was directed to the laundry where I got my prison issue underwear, uniforms, work boots, towels, toiletries and bedding. I was assigned to a room on the second floor of a three story dormitory/administration building. It was considered the "B" dorm. The room didn't have a lock or a catch on the door which surprised me, but it had six sets of bunk beds in approximately 300 square feet. Each occupant of the room also had a locker, stacked two high that also sucked up space. Two small desks were also part of the décor. My first thoughts were this facility is violating every fire code known to man and if even one of these guys picks up a germ, bug or virus the whole room could be infected.

The room I was first assigned to, had two other guys who were sixty-ish, five were white, two Hispanic and four Afro-American. Two of them were accountants and one a lawyer. Most of them claimed to believe in God and one was also Roman Catholic. I was actually quite fortunate to be assigned to this room as it was adjacent to the bathroom and showers. I made friends with everybody in the room and three of them were quite helpful in my getting acclimated. The staff person who was my "counselor" was of no help in the beginning.

One of the guys who was also an accountant, and had only a week left on his sentence, actually gave me a tour of the place and let me know where I had to be in the mornings, where the laundry, chapel, phone room and commissary were. It took ten days waiting for the counselor to explain the phone call process before one of my roommates showed me how to the use the phone system. My first call was to my wife to wish her a happy anniversary.

In October of 2008 the camp engaged in "ethnic cleansing", after deciding the rooms had to be racially balanced. They finally opened a separate drug dorm that was way over budget and way behind schedule. The BOP used "slave labor" to build it. Two brothers who were there did a great deal of the work. They should have named the building after them. The rooms in the other three dorms went down to ten inmates per room and were supposed to be four black, three white and three Hispanic. The room quickly became a place I stayed away from as long as I could. Cell phones were rampant, visitors camping out, card playing taking up space and all the guys I was close to had been moved. In February of 2009 I got a chance to move across the hall to a room that had rules, was quiet and had older guys in it. I jumped at it and one of the guys in the room, who became my bunkmate, went to the counselor and asked him to move me in. One of the guys in my old room told me to keep my mouth shut about what went on in the old room.

The Bureau of Prisons own manual says that inmates are supposed to have forty-five (45) square feet, not cubic feet, of space. In 2011, Wayne, a friend of mine challenged them about the overcrowding. His locker was subsequently raided. An ear piece with a volume control he used with his radio (that the commissary sold) was found and was considered "cell phone equipment" (i.e. contraband). Wayne was transferred to the county jail and then to another institution. I mentioned the space fact to a couple of the inmate-lawyers that I knew and gave them the citation and thought they should follow up but I don't know if they did. Somebody from the outside world needs to investigate this issue. Because this is a non-smoking facility, has fire alarms and smoke detectors somebody lets the BOP get away with what is obviously overcrowding. I never was able to determine whether county law, state law or Navy policy was supreme on this.

Non-violent?

Three weeks after I arrived at this "non-violent" offender institution an inmate named Ward Dean, a local doctor, was beaten up in the middle of the night. Mr. Dean was someone who knew Mr. Kahn and was there on a tax matter. A few days before the incident he introduced himself to me in the cafeteria. He was allegedly beaten with a combination lock wrapped up in a sock. His injuries included broken ribs, eye damage and numerous cuts. He was taken away by ambulance in the middle of the night and never came back to Pensacola. I thought to myself, so much for non-violent. The captain of the correction officers did suggest that nobody was safe as long as the perpetrator was unidentified. Eventually he was found out and left the camp cuffed and stuffed.

There were two other incidents of violence while I was at the camp. One involved a young black man who was on meds for psychological issues. He attacked an older inmate and two employees over a shower incident. It seems the older inmate tugged on the shower curtain while the younger inmate was using it. I didn't hear about there being anything malicious, just an accident that went out of control. The inmate was probably off his meds and probably shouldn't have been at this camp anyway. The inmate who was attacked went to the hospital for treatment and the other went to the county jail. Neither of the employees was seriously injured though a third inmate pulled the perpetrator off the female employee who was attacked trying to defuse the situation.

Another incident involved a gay inmate being assaulted.

Psych

All new inmates have to meet with the camp shrink to answer silly questions, some about being suicidal. I remember what one of the lawyers I worked with when I was a rookie accountant said, "I never met a shrink that didn't need one". The lady I had to meet with re-enforced his hypothesis. It was the only time I had to deal with her. Her "sentence" ran out before mine and she retired. Another consummate bureaucrat. I had to get the signature of the shrink who replaced her before I could be released. I never had any reason to interact with her so why did I need her permission to leave?

Visitation

The visitation area was certainly family friendly and no one had to sit behind a glass wall and use a hand phone, or visit via TV monitor. The place had a real community room complete with vending machines, TVs, cards and board games for kids. It didn't scream "prison" to those that came to visit other than the fact we all had to wear our green uniforms. The area also had a treed picnic area with a fence around it and amenities for kids. There were four TVs under a metal canopied area but no sound. Only inmates with special radios purchased from the camp could listen to the programming outside of visiting hours. From what I was told it was one of the nicest visiting areas in the entire system. My family and friends felt comfortable coming to visit.

Working the visiting room wasn't a favorite job for many of the employees. They actually had to work the seven hours a day of visitation each weekend. My mother came to visit thirty days after I got to Pensacola and then again about a year later. Both times the same employee was handling the check-in desk and both times it took him forty-five minutes to page me after my family was cleared. Both times my mother went to the desk and asked if I'd been paged. She was told I had been, but when I finally got there I assured her I hadn't been. She was going to write a complaint letter (which I encouraged her to do) but she was afraid there would be retaliation. Two of the employees that handled the check-in process were quite good at it. They got people in rather quickly and even recognized families that came regularly.

The first time I went to visitation there were two BOP officers checking the inmates in. One asked me "Where's Wesley going?" I looked at him and said "you work for the BOP and you're asking me?" He suggested I would know. How I would, I never understood. The other officer told me he knew my registration number, which dorm I was in and which bed I slept in. I asked him why I was so lucky that he knew all about me. He said it was just something was good at, remembering trivia.

There was an incident when my closest friend was taken to the hospital on a Friday night after fainting in the phone room. He hit his head and was bleeding so he was sent to the local hospital. The next morning his "significant other" showed up for visitation, having come five hours from Jacksonville, and was told he wasn't on the compound. Since they weren't "married" the BOP felt no obligation to tell her anything though she was probably his emergency contact person. When I showed up that morning for my visit with my family I asked the employee handling the check-in desk if she knew how my friend was and was told she couldn't talk about it. I made sure that my wife and the other lady exchanged contact information so that if a future incident occurred either might get some warning. More idiocy and lack of Christian decency.

Respect

The whole theme of prison life is to respect your fellow inmates' space, privacy, and property. Sadly too many of the inmates at this camp had the mentality that they were going to do what they wanted (engage in nefarious activity and handle contraband) and everybody else was going to keep their mouth shut and look the other way. Unfortunately that attitude created situations of group punishment for your roommates, co-workers or the facility in general. So much for respect. Troublemakers usually got transferred elsewhere, and farther from home. A lot inmates' had the attitude they could do their time anywhere. I remember one young Afro-American who was transferred to "Club Fed" and assigned to my room. He lasted about 3 days after being caught with a cell phone. His first reaction was "I'm just not feeling this place".

Punishment

One of my original roommates told me that the entire stay at "Club Fed" was all about the punishment.

Some of the added punishments we were subjected to as if being away from our families, living in overcrowded rooms, forced to work for 12 cents an hour in freezing weather as well as extreme heat, and middle of the night drug testing wasn't enough:

Being charged 23 cents a minute for long distance calls, 99 cents a minute for calls out of country (mostly Puerto Rico), limiting the phone usage to 300 minutes a month was/is also a form of punishment. The BOP was stealing from the families and monitoring the calls, so why not let them talk as much as they want. All this did was encourage the rampant use of cell phones that certainly didn't cost 99 cents a minute. If an inmate got caught he was transferred elsewhere and threatened with another year on his sentence. The general sentiment among those willing to take the risk was that "I can do my time anywhere". If a family was fortunate to buy themselves a cell phone with the local (850) area code then the cost of phone calls was only six cents a minute.

The winter of 2008 there was no heat in the B or C dorm. The air conditioner blower was working constantly and kept the room temperature at 54 degrees. While that may have kept down the spread of germs, it certainly could have caused pneumonia. I slept in sweat pants and thermal underwear, with sox on my feet many nights. The blankets the BOP issued were so thin and not solidly woven that they weren't much help. The fact that you had to make your bed every weekday morning made it almost impossible to sleep under the blankets. One inmate didn't want to disturb other inmates trying to make his bed in the morning. We slept on top of one blanket with a tissue thin sheet as a cover. Mysteriously in 2009 somebody figured out how to control the heat and the conditions improved. We did sleep on mattresses that were about 8" thick which came as a shock to me. Maybe the fact that we were at a slave labor camp, the BOP didn't want everybody crippled up from sleeping on 1" think foam mattresses.

The "A" dorm had constant hot water issue because of an aging and faulty boiler. The Navy finally fixed it in 2011. What nonsense.

Shakedowns, pat-downs and room searches were fairly common, some more often than others. In one incident the staff transferred an entire room to the county jail for a few days because no one claimed ownership of the multiple cell phones found in the room. So much for respecting your fellow roommates who weren't breaking the rules. So much for not punishing the many for the sins of the few. This facility did not have a "special housing unit" (SHU) so they contracted with the county to use its jail when they needed to punish certain activities. The county didn't allow for privacy, so when an inmate had to "answer the call of nature" they only had one toilet that multiple detainees had to share. My best friend got stuck there for eight-four days over an issue that was eventually dismissed by the disciplinary hearing officer. After being there eighty-four days what good was it? An inmate would lose his work assignment, room assignment, pittance of pay and visitor privileges. More abuse and again, no accountability.

All inmates not serving life sentences are entitled to 15% sentence reduction for good behavior. There seems to be a question as to how is fifteen percent computed? The BOP actually went all the way to the Supreme Court and the "Supremes" actually took up a case involving the computation of good behavior time.[21] Somebody who has passed fourth grade math would multiply the number of days in a year by. 15 and come up with the answer, that being 54. However, the BOP not wanting to be told what to do or how to run their prisons decided to use some of that "new math" and suggest inmates have to <u>earn</u> their good behavior time. The BOP will graciously give an inmate a fifteen percent sentence reduction for every day they behave. Using that mentality, fifteen percent becomes 47 days or thirteen and a half percent. The Justice Department has to cheat a lot of non-violent first time offenders out of a seven days a year just to "show 'em who's boss" and waste thousands of dollars in taxpayer money asking the "Supremes" (2010) to bless their arrogance. The states know how to compute fifteen percent. One would think that when there is lip-service given to a balanced budget and with the passage of a law to allow more halfway house and home confinement time that they would simply accept the spirit of those efforts and do the right thing. My solution is abolish all the low level prison facilities and let these "dangerous" criminals do real community service, put them in "electronic prisons", let the people working at these institutions collect unemployment and see if they can ever hold a real job.

An internet article entitled *"Prison Marriage, Can a Marriage Survive a Prison Sentence"*[22] suggested that 80% of all men's and 100% of women's marriages end in divorce. So much for "maintaining family ties" and re-integrating into society. If the federal prison system would wake up and allow conjugal visits they'd eliminate most of the mischief that goes on

---

[21]   Conrad Black, 2009, Honest Services case

[22]   Sheri Stritof,

in the lower security facilities and actually keep families together until all such **facilities are closed down permanently.**

"M", who I referred to in part one, was the victim of what is called "diesel-therapy" (being shuffled from facility to facility at a moments' notice) when the government said it needed him to be a witness in a related case. He spent 42 days being bounced from one jail to another while being transported to another part of the country. He did get a partial sentence reduction but paid a ridiculous price for it. It's a practice that should have been abolished decades ago. Another elderly inmate was subjected to this treatment as well yet was never called to testify. He did get a sentence reduction, but when I spoke with him he said it wasn't worth it.

Furloughs

BOP rules allow all minimum security inmates 30 days of furlough over the term of their sentence. That's time away from the facility to receive medical treatment beyond "basic" care, to attend funerals, to do job seeking, to renew family ties, go to job interviews, get a drivers' license renewed, apply for social security, and plan ahead with your family for life after prison. I didn't waste my breath asking for a furlough. The maximum for post imprisonment preparation was 5 days, but good luck trying to get that. The first warden at the camp suggested nobody needed a furlough just to have sex. I was going to back to northeastern Ohio to do my home confinement even though southwest Florida was my home area. I wanted to visit my elderly parents and the cost of a five day trip would have been prohibitive. I was eligible for social security and wasn't looking for a job. After three and half years of the idiocy what was five more days? When the five days were up, an inmate still had to come back.

Attending funerals was supposed to part of the 30 days also, but again good luck with that. Two of the guys I spent time with were denied a furlough to attend their mother's funeral even though such a request is allowable under BOP policy. One was denied because he hadn't been in the camp long enough. He was a low level white collar inmate with a sentence of about three years. He told the warden who denied his request, there was a special place in hell for people like him. The other inmate was Afro-American and was at a prison near Ocala when his mother died. His mother had lived in Cocoa Beach. The BOP claimed it was to close and too easy for him to escape. He was told to have the funeral video-taped and sent to him. He was a low level drug offender and being Afro-American probably didn't help his cause either. The BOP could have granted both requests and added the time missed to the end of their sentences. Neither would have objected, but hey "we're tough on crime".

Inmate Abuse

One of the guys I made friends with my first few days there was from Oregon. He told me had hadn't seen his family in two years. He has in prison on a drug charge and had originally been assigned to a prison camp in Arizona even though one in California was closer to his family. At the Arizona facility he had the job of "town driver". He drove other inmates to outside medical appointments, bus/train stations or airports when they were released. After being there 18 months and having good conduct, he was eligible for a transfer to another prison camp. The BOP sent him to Florida which was obviously farther away, because they could, and are never held accountable for such idiocy. So much for family ties! About a year before his sentence ran out he did get a transfer closer to home.

Three guys who worked with me actually lobbied to come to Pensacola because they had short sentences and when their lawyers did research they knew it was the place to be if you're going to get stuck anywhere. None of them should have been "in prison" anyway and could have done real community service instead of being pimped out to the Navy.

Several of the inmates were from Louisiana. One guy's wife came to visit almost weekly. She told him not only did he get sentenced but so did she. She had to travel, send him money, try to keep their business running and do without him for the time he was going to be incarcerated. He had a five year sentence that ended up being about thirty-tree months because of his participation in the BOP's drug program and the good behavior reduction.

Other than the six inmates who died while I was at the camp the most blatant case of abuse of an inmate I was aware of involved an inmate named Bob M. Bob went to prison for what the government called bank fraud. He had a fourteen year sentence. With good behavior, the drug program credit and halfway house time he *only* had to serve ten and a half years. From my perspective he was a model prisoner. On the very night before he was to be released to a halfway house in Southeast Florida he was given a "random" drug test. The results suggested he had crystal meth in his system. It was definitely a false reading influenced by some other medication the quack had given him for heart issues. Rather than order a second test or get the results from a real lab, or contact the quack, he was transferred to the county jail. He asked the employee who gave him the test how many other "random" tests were done that night and he was told "just you".

Bob's family contacted a high ranking rabbi in Palm Beach County who had contacts with the BOP. The rabbi contacted the local warden who claimed he didn't know anything about what happened, but sent a car to bring Bob back to the camp. Bob got stuck fourteen days in the county jail and a week at the camp before being released. When he was back at the camp I saw him in the cafeteria and asked him what exactly happened because prisons are great places for rumors and half-baked stories. I learned very early on that whenever an inmate had a story to tell the first words out of the listener's mouth should be "What's your source?" It is possible to have somebody on the outside with a computer verify any story within 24 hours.

Bob's wife died a few months before his release and this wasn't the only time he was deprived of eligible benefits. He had a contact in the publishing business and was also working on a book about his case and BOP experiences.

Commissary

The average inmate made $17 a month and that hasn't changed in 15 years. It doesn't go very far once you buy hygiene items. Overcharging, poor inventory control, limited hours and a ridiculously low spending limit were a constant problems for inmates. The BOP is stealing from the families and yet restricted what an inmate could spend and the prices they charge are excessive. The most blatant was the $6 charge for a case (12 cans) of soda. Primarily it was Coke products (regular, diet, Sprite). While being transported to work each day we would pass several convenient stores that advertised 3 for $11, 3 for $12, 4 for $12 for the same products. Were we supposed to believe that the BOP didn't have enough buying power to get better pricing? My last job was at the Navy's recycling plant on the base. Every week we would find surplus, thrown away flyers and ads put out by the Navy Exchange store. It also had pricing similar to the off base convenient stores. The inmates were told the BOP simply took its cost, added 30% and that's what the price was. How is it, the BOP was paying $4.60/ case for the same product? How did Coke manage to get away with charging $4.60/case? I smell a rat. Can you say price gouging? Kickbacks?

After I left the camp I wanted to buy the brand of potato chip the commissary sold because I thought they tasted good. What I found is that company was Canadian and did not distribute potato chips to the general public, strictly to the BOP. What? We can't support American businesses?

A major supplier of products to the BOP was a company known as "Keefe". They are not a publicly traded company and finding out who really owns it is something every inmate would like to know. The obvious answer we think is some politically connected family.

The BOP was gracious enough not to profiteer off the stamps they sold but would only sell them on Monday nights. Why? It's a commodity just like anything else they sold. The commissary was only open three days for food and hygiene items and only on Monday for clothing, shoes and boots. Why? Maybe it's a union thing.

Every three months the commissary put out a new list of products as items they sold and suppliers did change. The officer in charge made a point to insist that inmates only take one list. Yet while working at the recycling plant I had an occasion to empty a trailer full of paper. It was from the camp and had well over 1,000 obsolete commissary sheets. Just more idiocy and waste.

The commissary process was such that an inmate dropped his list inside and then stood outside waiting for his name to be called. In December of 2008 some of us had to stand outside in the cold and wind for about an hour waiting to get the things we ordered. I ended up with a cold that lasted about 10 days. The cold room temperature didn't help my recovery and the commissary did not sell any cold remedies. They did sell generic versions of Claritin, Tylenol and Robitussin. Drink lots of water was the standard "prescription". I sucked down all the Vitamin C pills I had and ate as many oranges as I could find but I never went to the commissary on cold days again.

About a year and a half before my time expired, the BOP actually opened up a second check out window that speeded up the process. God only knows why they couldn't have done it all along. I guess we weren't being punished enough. The commissary also felt the effect of the depression that hit the real world because it became faster to get in and out of the commissary the last year of my stay. I made a comment about that to a guy who worked in the commissary and he admitted the families were broke and couldn't send as much money so the commissary didn't sell as much.

Besides clothes, boots, shoes, hygiene and food products the camp sold wrist watches. Twice I had to replace the battery in mine. The first time the inmates staffing the commissary put the battery in for me. The second time I handed the camp employee my watch thinking they would put the battery in. I was sarcastically told this wasn't a watch store. The camp did not sell watch repair equipment and according to the employee manual we are all given they day we arrive, one inmate is not allowed to give another inmate anything. So how are you supposed to install the battery? Luckily a resourceful inmate with eyeglass repair kit installed my battery.

All of the "profits" generated from commissary sales allegedly go into an "Inmate Trust Fund". Being an inmate I made a written request for a copy of the annual audit of this "fund" shortly before I was released. I wasn't given the courtesy of any response. I then sent my request to Washington. That too was ignored. According to an inmate who worked in the commissary, the weekly sales averaged $10,000. That suggests over $150,000 a year is put into a fund for the benefit of inmates. Rumor had it the money was spent primarily on recreational activities and related equipment, however the people it is supposed to benefit have no idea what actually happens to it.

Staff/Counselors/case managers

Each inmate is assigned someone with the title "counselor" and "case manager". They had four of each at the camp. I think overpaid, paycheck stealing bureaucrats pretty much sums up what they were. The first thing I went to my counselor about was the fact that the boots I was issued were very uncomfortable even though they were new. His august advice was to try two pair of socks. What he didn't tell me was that I had the option of trading the boots in for a pair of used boots (if they had my size). After suffering for 3 weeks even with two pair of socks, another inmate told me about used boots. I went to the laundry and though they didn't have anything in my size they did have a pair of size a half size bigger that seemed to run small and they were wonderful. I got almost 18 months wear out of them and didn't really want to give them up but the heel was just about gone. After that the only thing I did "ask/apply" from my counselor for was a "vacation", and that was towards the end of my "tour of duty".

All incoming inmates have to attend an orientation class. It's actually part of a checklist of items that need to be completed. The day of my orientation class one of the speakers was the Afro-American counselor assigned to the "A" dorm. He made it very clear he hadn't done anything in twenty years and was only ninety-two days away from his release (i.e. retirement) and he wasn't about to start now. If you looked up "consummate bureaucrat" in a dictionary you'd probably find his picture instead of a definition. From what chatter I picked up around at the camp and from guys I worked with or ate meals with not one of them was overjoyed with their counselor either.

When it came to case managers I had four of them. The first one got transferred to the new "drug dorm". The second one retired. Did her time and boogied. The third one was simply filling the vacancy temporarily and the fourth one was still there when I left. I only saw the first 3 once each (which was too much) and the fourth one I was stuck with every three months. None of my meetings with these people lasted more than five minutes and a couple only three. I didn't have any fines to pay or any restitution and I already had an education and I wasn't interested in learning Spanish so they had nothing to offer or require of me. I did avail myself of the last one's services to request a presidential pardon. The unit manager at the time who was sitting in on the meeting had to inform me of how few are actually granted (unless you have connections like a few of Clinton's cronies). I knew I had a snowball's chance in hell of getting one but it did make them actually do a little work and earn a few pennies of their paychecks. I'm certain when I listed that we had a tax cheat running the Treasury and formerly the House Ways and Means Committee (who were never prosecuted) in my application as two of the reasons I deserved a pardon didn't help my cause either.

I did make a written request to my last case manager asking what the "successful re-integrating into society" part of the BOP's "mission statement" meant. She wrote back and said getting a job (i.e. some kind on income stream) and obeying the law was a start. That suggests if a person was mopping out toilets and stocking shelves for minimum wage at some fast food establishment and not exceeding the speed limits they had re-integrated. The fact that a person may not own a car, was living under a bridge, begging food, couldn't pay utilities, or lacked health insurance didn't matter. Forget the fact that his ties with his family may have been destroyed. But hey what can you expect from someone stealing a paycheck and parroting government idiocy.

Cafeteria

The food the BOP served could be described as fair to good. The budget was allegedly under $3/inmate/day. The BOP tried to make a big deal on holidays but they only fed us twice on those days, though they did allow doggie bags. The camp did have a salad bar (which was unheard of in the prison system) but having salad dressing was never a guarantee. Breakfast and lunch were eatable, I can't say as much for the dinners, most of which I skipped my last year there. The theft (especially eggs and vegetables) both by staff and inmates was unacceptable. Some inmates' saw it as a way of getting even with the BOP for abusing them. Quite a few of the food boxes said "made in China" or "for inmate use only". So much for supporting American farmers/businesses. But farmers didn't lend us a trillion dollars to help fund wasteful programs like this camp.

Slave Labor Camp/Job Assignments

The principal source of punishment was the fact that PFC-Pensacola was a slave labor camp which we were reminded of in nauseating detail numerous times. The basic wage was 12 cents an hour and the pay scale ranged from $17 a month to $400 a month. The highest paying jobs involved working for a Unicor facility at the Air Force Base at Eglin, Florida. The majority of the inmates made the minimum.

Unicor and the inmates who worked there made clothing for military people. Those jobs went to people with court ordered restitution and the prison system took half their pay as payment on that restitution. There were the usual "on base" jobs: laundry, commissary, kitchen, maintenance and dorm orderlies. I didn't want to be on the base even though those jobs paid more money. Being away from the camp diminished the sense that you were "incarcerated". The off-base jobs included Unicor, a golf course, Eglin Air Force Base, the recycling plant, Corey Station (part of NAS) and the main base at the Naval Air Station (known as DZ). Inmates were loaded on tour buses (driven by inmates), school buses, or mini-vans and driven by unarmed retired military people to other parts of the Naval Air Station each morning.

The plum job at the camp was that of the chaplain's clerk. That job came with an air-conditioned office and a TV with all the cable channels. Since the chaplain worked a forty hour week just like all the rest of the staff, the clerk's job had fringe benefits. There were four clerks during my time, only one of which was Catholic. One was "a-religious" and never attended any service conducted there. I thought there were more deserving/qualified individuals and said so, but there is no understanding the idiocy of bureaucrats.

Through the grace of God I was never assigned a job at Eglin Air Force Base. It required those inmates to get up before 5 AM, try to use the showers and toilets at the same time 200 other guys were. They were allowed to be first in line for breakfast and but practically had to inhale the food so they could be at the bus loading area by 5:30. The buses finally pulled out about 6 AM. The inmates had a 75 minute bus ride to Eglin Air Force Base. It was a three bus caravan driven by inmates with one officer in a BOP vehicle as an "escort". While it was a full size tour bus the seats didn't allow room for tall people, or large people, or guys who wanted to recline the seat and nap. The buses did have a DVD player and movies were shown on the trip back. The food they got for lunch was left over from the day before at the camp and bordered on garbage. These inmates got back to the camp at 4:45 each day and could go right to the chow hall. By the time they ate, got a shower, went to commissary, got their mail or went to a religious service their day was shot and it was time to go to bed and start the routine all over. They did get paid "travel time" but it wasn't any compensation for the extra hours and lousy food.

I spent my first three weeks at the camp doing raking and trash pickup. Then I was sent to an off-base job site and spent two days sitting at a picnic table waiting to be interviewed for a more permanent assignment. My first outside assignment was on a 7-man grass cutting crew that was responsible for the grounds at the naval hospital in Pensacola. Four of the guys were white, two black and one Hispanic and it was a great crew. My primary job was to push a street blower around behind the guys that cut and edged the lawns. It involved a lot of walking but we only worked from 8 to 10:30 each morning. We ate lunch from 11:00 to noon and then picked up trash around the grounds after lunch. We spent half an hour looking for trash and staying out of the way the rest of the time. I didn't mind the work but it was the midst of the summer heat and 90 degrees plus was not fun. We did have plenty of water and there was plenty of shade. The Navy "black-flagged" the base if the heat index got over 100 degrees but the public address warning didn't seem to apply to the inmates. That did change when the warden at the time ('08 & '09) was transferred.

Our supervisor was a former Army veteran which was strange because most of the other employees of the company that supervised our work were ex-Navy. One of the other supervisors at this assignment was from my home town in Ohio. My boss was Afro-American, a devote Christian, husband and father. He was also the ultimate fanatical Alabama fan. I think he was in his late 50's and knowing the country had been at peace for the years he was probably in the service I asked him one day if he "saw any action". Without hesitating or skipping a beat he said, "Yeah, I was coming out of the barracks one day and there were two dogs going at it on the front lawn". My only regret about working for him was that I wasn't sitting next to him in January, 2009, the night Utah beat up on Alabama in the Sugar Bowl. Utah went undefeated and deserved to be national champs but the Bowl Championship people didn't see it that way. My boss agreed that Utah was #1.

I had three other jobs at this work area, one of which involved working outside and two that were inside most of the time. I cut grass, trimmed grass, edged grass, pulled weeds, trimmed bushes, cleaned fence lines, fixed sprinkler systems, manned a gas pump, kept up a supply of mixed gas, cleaned bathrooms, collected trash, spray painted stencils/signs, signed out tools and was probably the "MVP" of the Corey Station detail. That's "Most Versatile Prisoner". Whatever odd job needed done I got stuck with it.

One day I had to chauffer the construction crew to their designated work area because no one on that crew had a "prison drivers' license". I don't know why I was given one, but I drove a six-pack pickup truck out the front gate of the maintenance area and turned left. Thirty feet later I turned left again into a parking lot and drove off the parking lot to a fence line at the edge of the base property, got out of the truck and walked back to the maintenance garage. The crew was allowed to operate pickup truck off road. At lunch time I walked back and drove the crew back to the maintenance building. What a joke.

I also spent four weeks on a tree cutting crew that was supposed to be some kind of punishment because it was outside work and it was December. The boss and I got along well and he was on vacation for two of the four weeks I was assigned to his detail. He even gave me a raise after only a week on the job. Having arthritis in my wrists I didn't feel of capable of handling chain saws and hedgers and I got transferred to the recycling plant.

One of the hurricanes that went through the Florida panhandle in 2005 wiped out the building the recycling plant formerly used. They were now using a rat-infested, poorly insulated metal building that had no heat and was filthy. The work was dirty to. It was a 7 man detail. I spent most of the time recycling aluminum cans and plastic bottles most of which came to the plant in trash hoppers or bags and I never knew what was in them. It was the dirtiest job in the plant but also the easiest.

The building did have a couple of space heaters that were used to generate some heat in the winter. One of them was kept in the restroom with the door closed so it would warm up on really cold mornings. I learned how to operate a forklift, a paper shredding line, a plastic baler, a can baler and a wire stripper. I also swept and pressure washed the floors, stripped wire, and wrapped paper bales in my spare time. The boss was a great guy to work for.

One of the few fringe benefits of working at Pensacola Naval Air Station was the free air show we got during the week. PNAS was the home of the Navy's Blue Angels, and they practiced right over the base for the aerial shows they put on around the country. While I'm sure it's a great show and a nice way to "serve your country" the cost still comes under the heading of "national defense" and the dirtbags in Washington claim we can't cut the defense budget. And yes the cost of this unit may be "chump change" in the whole scheme of things but those planes aren't cheap, they burn a lot of fuel, have a lot of support teams and you probably have to be at least a captain to fly one. To help with the budget they agreed to reduce the numbers of days that they practiced from three to two.

As a way to cut their budget the BOP cut the pay of all the inmates who worked off base either at the Naval Air Station, Whiting Field, Eglin Air Force Base, Corey Station and the re-cycling plant. For those of us making "minimum wage" (i.e. 12 cents an hour) there was no cut, but for the guys making $60 a month it was a big deal. Many of them could no longer make phone calls, buy stamps, use the internet or buy food. However all the inmates who worked on base (kitchen, laundry, maintenance, recreation, orderlies) did not see a cut. Why? Yet "everybody is treated the same", or so my counselor tried to tell me.

Having never been in the military I looked on my time at Club Fed as a substitute. I spent three and a half years pimped-out to the Navy to maintain their properties. I had to shake my head over the thought that some of our supervisors who were ex-military were somehow keeping us safe.

A young Spanish guy who worked with me at my first assignment at Corey Station asked me what I thought of prison life. I told him "if I ever get to one I'll let you know". Pensacola was called "Prisneyland", a Boy Scout camp, an adult day care center, and a slave labor camp besides "Club Fed". Ninety percent of the inmates should never have been there and 10% should never get out.

Drug Program

The most sought after perk at FPC Pensacola was the infamous "drug program". The technical moniker was "RDAP" which is what was on a red label above the shirt pocket of each inmate who was enrolled in the program. That was an acronym for the "Residential Drug and Alcohol Program". Another possibility bantered around was "Really Dumb Ass Prisoner". Take your pick because I never saw so many grown men grovel to get into a program that humiliated them in exchange for time off.

Before beginning my time I did some research on the net about "surviving" your stay in prison. While Pensacola was nothing of what I envisioned a prison to be, one of the sites I visited said to enroll in the drug and alcohol program because it guaranteed an inmate a year off their sentence and six months at a halfway house. That is in addition to the good behavior credit inmates earn. Since I never touched an illegal drug in my life, never smoked anything, and what alcohol I consumed in my life wouldn't keep a tavern open for an hour I had no idea how'd I'd even qualify. Because of all the incentives no one was eligible for the program until they got within three years (later 42 months) of their release date. As I remember Michael Vick transferred from a camp he was originally assigned to one in the Midwest because it had the RDAP program. I think his sentence was too short to do him any good.

My first quandary was that if an inmate had a "drug problem" at the time he was convicted or arrived at the prison why the hell did he have to wait months and even years to get "treatment". One of the guys I knew, Gene, had a fifteen year sentence involving drugs but no drug problem, yet the BOP didn't "treat" his "problem" until he got down to his last three years. Most of the other inmates considered the drug program people "chosen ones" because they had to apply for the program, allegedly demonstrate a problem and then get approved. Successful graduates allegedly earned the BOP a $2,500 bounty from the Department of Education. They wanted as many applicants as possible. Isn't this really one bunch of bureaucrats subsidizing another bunch?

What they considered treatment were just classes and group meetings about what bad decisions you made, and how your "substance abuse problem" contributed to your "criminal behavior". The BOP abandoned the 'RDAP" labels and changed to multi-colored lancets that participants wore around their neck so they were easily identifiable (almost like the scarlet letter). They worked at jobs around the camp. Paycheck stealing bureaucrats are running this program and they talk to inmates about criminal behavior. Believe me they couldn't get a job in the real world. Writing your autobiography and living together in the same dorm where outsiders weren't allowed was also part of the program. Group punishment was also common when someone violated a sacred rule or was caught with contraband. The program took nine and a half months to complete after which there was a formal graduation ceremony.

Even though the website I found the information said a one year reduction, Pensacola didn't seem to get the memo because in July, 2008 no one was getting more than six months off for completing the program. Was that additional punishment? One of the guys who worked with me at Corey Station actually applied for and was granted a transfer to the prison camp in McKeon, PA in January, 2009 (the same place Wesley Snipes was assigned to) because that facility was giving their drug program graduates a year off. The guy was from the Boston area anyway and would have been closer to home when he was released and less of a burden on his family to visit. By July of 2010 Pensacola got in line with the rest of the country.

One of the RDAP guys was from the same town as I and was my poster child for working the system. While the $400,000 he spent on lawyer fees didn't get him acquitted, he did learn all the right answers to all the questions to get into the drug program. He admitted to using cocaine and drinking excessively. I don't believe either one of those was true but it worked. He showed up at Pensacola in July, 2009 with a 41 month sentence and left just days before Christmas, 2010. He served less than 50% of his sentence. No other inmate I knew of got out so fast.

Most of the guys I associated with who were in the drug program probably didn't have a drug or alcohol problem. One of them told me, "I don't owe these people the truth".

The first day I spent sitting at a picnic table waiting for a job assignment I met an elderly black inmate who was close to the end of his "vacation" and who had been there over some nonsensical tax matter. He had about as much love for the IRS as I do - NONE. Since I was new we got to talking and the subject of the drug program came up. When I told him I probably wouldn't qualify he said to me, three times "You drink don't you?" I finally got his point. There really wasn't any yardstick to verify someone's alleged substance or alcohol abuse. The six months off wasn't enough of an incentive for me, considering the extra benefit that should have been provided by the recently enacted Second Chance Act of 2007.

If an inmate had a long sentence (5 years or more) what the heck is six months. (In hindsight I'm glad I didn't get the extra time for the halfway house either because that place sucked. It was another waste of taxpayer money.) The BOP should have given inmates who didn't have drug and alcohol addiction the extra benefit of the Second Chance Act as a reward for not having those bad habits, and not developing them while in prison. But they weren't getting a bounty from those kind of inmates.

Waste

The work assignment I had for my last 11 months in the rat infested recycling plant at the Naval Air Station was a real first-hand look at waste. My first job was to man a paper shredding line. I would shred newspaper, magazines, books and pamphlets the Navy wasted money on. The Navy had printed soft bound manuals for low altitude U.S. radar instrument approved minimums. They had a different manual for each part of the country. Every 60 days they became obsolete and were sent to recycling. Boxes upon boxes, many never opened. The Navy also wasted money on pamphlets about educational opportunities and medical benefits. I shredded thousands of pieces of these, all in boxes and still wrapped in plastic. (Wouldn't you love to have a government printing contract?) There was also a stack of boxes of books, 16 pallets in all, with 16 boxes per pallet and 4 hard bound books per box that were unopened. The books were "Guide to the Evaluation of Educational Experiences in the Armed Services 1954-1989". The boxes had been laying around a long time. Each book has just page after page of listing of courses available. I often wondered how many trees the military killed and how much money they waste overprinting. In the scheme of government waste it was "chump change", but they could only afford to pay me 12 cents an hour.

Another piece of genius I encountered while working at the recycling plant, was when some rocket scientist got the hair-brained idea that shredding documents etc. wasn't good enough so they changed the grinding wheels on the shredder so that the paper would be pulverized. No one could have ever pieced the shredded documents back together and yet the air was now being filled with paper dust and the workers had to wear a dust mask to breathe while working. <u>Insanity at its finest</u>. Just before I left the camp the Navy inspector shut down that part of the building because of asbestos in the walls. I guess he missed the rats.

A true national disgrace is the number of homeless and unemployed veterans in this country. Another feature that "60 Minutes" aired, in 2011, was about a mini-convention in southern California of 963 such vets from all around the country. They were seeking various forms of aid and assistance and the people that arranged the gathering were trying to counsel them on how to get help.

While watching the program I thought about what a waste of time PFC Pensacola was, how 90% of us should never have been there and how grateful most of those 963 homeless vets would be to have a real bed to sleep in, even if it meant sharing with 11 other people, and having a hot shower daily. I'm certain they wouldn't have minded working the kitchen, laundry or being janitors in exchange and wouldn't have complained about "overcrowding". A lot of them probably had more of a drug problem than the guys who were enrolled in the camp's drug program. These people put their ass on the line for this country and yet we spend money building prisons and ignoring them. Pensacola isn't the only institution that needs to go, especially when we have veterans who need help. And no, society would not be any more at risk if this camp changed uses, though I often teased some of my fellow inmates about how much better my family slept knowing they were in prison. What a joke.

The place is a $12-15M/year waste of money, a large portion of which was buried under "national defense" since the Navy is/was paying a private civilian contractor (RSSI Inc.) to maintain its grounds and the contractor was using slave labor (inmates) leased from the BOP to do the work. The guy who dreamed it up deserves a pat on the back and somebody is getting rich off it.

It seems one federal agency can't do "business" directly with another agency so somebody created a very profitable intermediary. "Keep the buses rolling" was allegedly the camp motto, as the BOP wanted to be sure they fulfilled their end of the contract. This particular camp was one of two "stand-alone" camps in the BOP System. The other was at Maxwell AFB in Alabama. Both of them should have been shut down long ago.

Who says we can't cut the defense budget? I realize $15 million doesn't run the government for much more than two minutes but aren't there better ways to waste the money. Ask those homeless vets. Couldn't they waste it on you? Then again maybe they are. Why can't the inmates do real community service and let the Navy use its own personnel to maintain its property. It could be their form of punishment for bad behavior. The civilian contractors didn't appreciate inmates taking work away from them either.

The third warden that was assigned to this facility (the BOP plays musical wardens every two years) wanted a door buzzer on his office to prevent staff from walking in unannounced and a new conference table made of mahogany. A guy that I knew who worked in the carpentry shop said the wood cost $8,000. He even had a few scraps left to make a cabinet for the chaplain's clerk office. The inmates also assisted in building a lighted fountain monument in the parking lot in memory of fallen prison employees. Unfortunately only the staff and the inmates ever saw it and the alleged $40,000 cost couldn't be justified. Chicken feed to a government that wastes billions every day but it was probably already in the budget and had to be spent.

Second Chance Act of 2007

In April of 2008 about a week before my sentencing hearing President Bush signed into law legislation affectionately called "The Second Chance Act of 2007". Then *Senator* Joe Biden was actually a co-sponsor of this bill. It was a classic piece of garbage legislation. Two of more important provisions of the bill as seen from the inmates' prospective were the increase from six months to one year the total time an inmate can spend at a halfway house and on home detention at the completion of their sentence. The intent was to help with prison overcrowding and save money. But sadly it was just a concept. The "rocket scientists" who wrote the bill used the word "discretion" (of the BOP) when talking about the additional time an inmate could spend as an alternative to incarceration. The BOP saw it as a threat to their jobs and the case managers feared if they signed off on an inmate's release and the person committed another crime, especially a violent crime, they would be "called on the carpet" and made to justify their actions. Sadly the fallout from former Gov. Mike Huckabee's reducing the sentence of a state inmate, who later committed a serious crime, was fresh in their minds. The other benefit was to provide post-release training and job searching assistance of about $150 million. Unfortunately Congress never funded those programs.

Even worse was the arrogant attitude of former BOP director Harley Lappin that no inmate needed more than six months to find a job and re-integrate into society even in the midst of the worst economic conditions since the Great Depression. After Mr. Lappin was replaced the attitude continued. The BOP claimed they make their decisions on a "case-by-case" basis. The fact that not one of the more than 30,000 inmates in the federal minimum security facilities (camp system) was worthy of the additional time validates their arrogance. I guess the inmates still haven't been punished enough!

Hundreds of inmates all over the country, including several of my friends at Club Fed were filing habeas corpus motions when it became apparent the BOP couldn't care less what Congress intended, they had "discretion", and were going to do what they damn well pleased. I read many of those filings, helped research a couple and typed one. Even though they were legally sound, on point and cited relevant cases besides the actual law, the courts paid little respect to pro-se filings and refused to order any inmates released, simply sending an occasional case back to the BOP for "reconsideration". One attorney/inmate told me the court had "eviscerated" the BOP in one such opinion. I read the case when it came through the camp, and confronted the attorney and asked him what case he was reading.

For the record the law said inmates should be given time that would provide the GREATEST LIKELYHOOD OF SUCCESSFUL REINTEGRATION INTO SOCIETY (excerpt below). Obviously that could vary from inmate to inmate but "one size fits all" doesn't work. The main character in a TV drama called *Bones* made a comment during an episode in 2012: ".. when people have blind subservience to institutional authority their judgment is often compromised". Translation: Contrary to common practice and belief in the government circles, *ONE SIZE DOES NOT FIT ALL.*

Since "this is prison and EVERYBODY is treated the same" (as per my illustrious counselor) how does one rationalize three months of halfway house time on a fifteen month sentence; (John B., Dean R.), five months (Shorty) on an eighteen month sentence, or even six months on a three year or fifteen year sentence. Clearly everybody wasn't being treated the same.

(3) ASSISTANCE- The United States Probation System shall, to the extent practicable, offer assistance to a prisoner during prerelease custody under this subsection.

(4) NO LIMITATIONS- Nothing in this subsection shall be construed to limit or restrict the authority of the Director of the Bureau of Prisons under section 3621.

(5) REPORTING- Not later than 1 year after the date of the enactment of the Second Chance Act of 2007 (and every year thereafter), the Director of the Bureau of Prisons shall transmit to the Committee on the Judiciary of the Senate and the Committee on the Judiciary of the House of Representatives a report describing the Bureau's utilization of community corrections facilities. Each report under this paragraph shall set forth the number and percentage of Federal prisoners placed in community corrections facilities during the preceding year, the average length of such placements, trends in such utilization, the reasons some prisoners are not placed in community corrections facilities, and any other information that may be useful to the committees in determining if the Bureau is utilizing community corrections facilities in an effective manner.

(6) ISSUANCE OF REGULATIONS- The Director of the Bureau of Prisons shall issue regulations pursuant to this subsection not later than 90 days after the date of the enactment of the Second Chance Act of 2007, which shall ensure that placement in a community correctional facility by the Bureau of Prisons is--

(A) conducted in a manner consistent with section 3621(b) of this title;

(B) determined on an individual basis; and

(C) of sufficient duration to provide the greatest likelihood of successful reintegration into the community.'.

(b) Courts May Not Require a Sentence of Imprisonment to Be Served in a Community Corrections Facility- Section 3621(b) of title 18, United

Chapel/Chaplain

I was surprised that this camp had a Catholic priest as the chaplain, but I was very disappointed in him. I've known, served mass for and talked with many priests in my sixty plus years as a Catholic. He didn't meet my expectations. He stood at the pulpit one Sunday and made it quite clear about the he hadn't taken any vow of poverty and was a BOP employee (i.e. cop). That's all I needed hear. He was also counting down the days to the end of his sentence. It seems besides allowing its employees to steal their paychecks *they have to retire* at age 57 and are eligible to collect 50-80% of their salary as a pension. Those of us receiving moneys from the giant Ponzi scheme saw our retirement age raised to 67 and the minimum benefits don't come close to 50% of our income.

When the chaplain's clerk asked me to pinch hit as an altar server one Sunday I declined. The chaplain had some health issues and retired in July, 2009 about the same time as the shrink. I knew the BOP was not going to appoint another priest to be the chaplain here. While 175 of the 800 inmates claimed to be Catholic less than 50 attended services. Though the retiring chaplain allegedly looked for another Catholic priest to come and celebrate mass there is a major shortage of priests and finding one who could come on Sunday was impossible. We were honored at Christmas in 2010 that the local bishop came to the camp to celebrate mass.

In November, 2009 the pastor at a Catholic church less than one mile from the camp was excited about ministering at the camp after one of the inmate's wives told him about the need. So where did the former chaplain look? Unfortunately the new priest could only come on Wednesday night, but "beggars can't be choosers".

Father John had been ordained late in life and we were truly blessed to have him. He had been in the music industry prior to becoming a priest and actually provided some entertainment as well as celebrating mass.

He held a concert open to the whole camp just before I left. He "made some noise" as he called it and was well received.

When "M" was released in July, 2010 I took over as the altar assistant and was deemed the spokesperson for the Catholic contingency when the time came for an "audit" by the national office. I did an interview with the national chaplain in August of 2011 as part of his "audit" of the prison chaplaincy. The "audit" consisted of four trivial questions about the chaplain and if he was accessible and available to all denominations. While I find it commendable that the BOP respects an inmates' right to worship and pray and that while incarcerated many of them find God, my question is "Why doesn't the government do more to put God into their lives before they got there?"

When the chaplain asked me if I had any questions, I said I wanted to know why Good Friday wasn't designated as a religious day for the Christians and a day inmates wouldn't have to work considering those who were Muslims had every Friday off as part of their religious beliefs. I was told that we should take the matter up with a higher authority and that he didn't see why it couldn't be granted. When I brought the issue up with the local chaplain he suggested the decision was that of the assistant warden and since she didn't get Good Friday off she didn't she why inmates should. What nonsense. I wasn't going to be there the next year anyway but I told the rest of the guys to follow up on it.

In the first quarter of 2011 the new chaplain mysteriously had money in his budget to spend. The Catholic service needed some new cruets for the water and wine and a small table to them and a chalice on. I'm sure both items could have been bought at Walmart for less than $100. The guys who worked the wood shop probably could have made a table out of scraps from the warden's fancy mahogany conference table. The cruets the chaplain ordered were a fancy glass and cost about $160. The table was also $160 unassembled and would have been $300 assembled. I was also given a catalog of Catholic books, catechisms and videos and was able to order whatever I thought the library needed. I marked about

20 items that cost about $300. I hope somebody used them or read them. One other purchase made by the chaplain was a movie screen with accompanying overhead projector that was installed in the chapel. It was intended to show religious themed movies once a week but the attendance was rather weak. It was another waste of money, but again "chump change" in terms of government spending/waste.

While the building housing the chapel and the psych department had a restroom for inmate use, there was a "turf war" over when it was available. It was locked more than it was open. What good is it to have house for prayer and meditation open to all but not allowing the use of the restroom? Seems it was on the side of the building that was used primarily by the "psych" department/RDAP program and they decided they could decide when the restroom would be open. Just another reason why I called this book dirtbags, liars and power freaks.

Mail

The camp had three different systems for mail delivery while I was there. The last two were outside, rain or shine, hot or cold. Originally you just showed up in your dorm at 6:30 and wait for your name to be called, meaning you had mail. Most of the time the person(s) handing out mail would start calling names alphabetically starting with "A" but sometimes started with "Z" trying to be fair. After the first two systems bombed somebody decided to create a list of names and use a highlighter to let us know if we had mail. The list was posted outside the chow hall. Pick up was still outside but at least you didn't have to waste your time standing around only to find you didn't get anything. The lady who passed out the mail was well liked and was very good at the job, remembered names and faces and moved the process along. She eventually gave it up which was unfortunate. I remember standing at the window to get my mail when she saw another inmate across the parking lot who hadn't collected his mail lately and she yelled out to him to come and get his mail. I looked up at her and said "Ma'am could you yell a little louder I don't think they heard you in Mobile!" She waved her hand as if she wanted to swat me. I reminded her these are grown men, she shouldn't be coddling them.

Staff

I didn't talk to any of the employees that I wasn't forced to. Though I did ask one of the "correction officers" why he was still working when it was obvious he was able to retire. He said quote "My country needs me". I said to him "You're full of shit". To which he said "that's what happens when you hang around a place like this for 19 years". He was the poster child of a consummate paycheck stealing bureaucrat, but I admired him for working the system. I think the fact that he had a few bad habits (cigarettes and beer) and kids may actually be why he had to keep working.

A relatively new young officer who was handling check-ins at visitation one Sunday when my family came asked me why I was there. I gave my pat answer, "me and the IRS have a hate/hate relationship". A month or so later I saw the same officer in the chapel corridor and asked him the same question, "Why are YOU here?" His response was "that's a good question". I saw him again on the day before I was released and told him to find another career before he got much older.

Education

The education department was, at best obsolete and at worst just a vehicle to get additional federal agencies to subsidize the operation of the camp. Making sure inmates who didn't have a high diploma got one was their hot button. One of the guys I knew was 70 years old and had been paratrooper in the military, a successful tax consultant/tax planner as well as a businessman in Texas and was smarter than most of the people employed at the camp. Unfortunately for him the high school he attended burnt down many years ago and most of the records including his were lost. It didn't stop the military from accepting him or him risking his life. Since he couldn't produce a diploma and but old enough for social security he still got stuck attending the classes. When I saw him wearing his cap and gown at the "graduation" event I asked him why he was there and he told me the whole story. Just goes to show you no one working for the government is allowed to think for themselves or "buck the system", but they made $500. The joke around the camp was that you didn't need a high school diploma to get hired but you did need one to get out.

Miscellaneous Idiocy

"Diesel therapy" is a very common form of inmate abuse and should be abolished. There is no justification to bounce and inmate from place to place, jail to jail especially when you're seeking their cooperation. It's bad enough they send them cuffed and stuffed. When the inmate finally gets to their final destination or back to their original facility they have to wait days to get THEIR property (clothes, shoes, hygiene items, photos, letters) back even though that property was inspected and packed by BOP personnel and handled by BOP throughout their trip. What? are there unscrupulous people collecting a government paycheck in the prison system? I guess you haven't been punished enough and if you were getting a sentence reduction they want to cram all the punishment they can into your last days. One elderly inmate (Ed R.) was stuck for 6 weeks in a rat-infested federal detention center on the pretext he was going to be a witness for the government. He never did testify but got a sentence reduction anyway. The abuse may not have been worth it. Why couldn't they have taken him by plane a day before they actually needed him rather than transfer him to a dump and let him wonder what was going on?? But NOBODY is accountable and inmates are considered lower than pond scum.

My entire detail was stripped search upon returning from work one day back in '09. Seems somebody got a tip that contraband was being smuggled. They didn't find anything.

The camp also had a metal detector that all of us that worked off the compound had to pass thru when returning from work. But when it broke sometime in 2010 they never fixed or replaced it. Must have been a real valuable asset. Rumor was it was originally bought to screen the employees.

There were numerous false alarm fire drills while I was at the camp. Several of them came from a malfunctioning electronic equipment in the administration section of the building. It's hard enough to sleep in these places without constantly being awaken by a fire alarm. On one occasion the alarm went off three times in a row. No sooner had we been herded back inside and it went off again. It was chalked up to inmate mischief. So much for respect for your fellow inmates.

RECREATION

The camp did have an outdoor covered weight pile, a <u>lighted</u> bocce ball court, a regulation softball field, a walking/jogging track, a movie theater (that was later closed) the Navy allowed us to use, a basketball court, a leisure library, a card/game room and plenty of TVs. The lights on the bocce ball court came under the heading of waste. They also built a fancy scorer's tower for the softball field, a new 6' chain-link fence and bought uniforms to be used when a camp team played a local area team. But inmates had to go to work hurt, couldn't get proper tests, treatment or medication. Go figure where their priorities were.

Exit Runaround

When my time was finally at an end I couldn't leave without one last dose of nonsense. The day before my release I had to wander from department to department (it's SOP) and get an autograph from the department head giving me permission to leave. I had nothing to do with most of these people, didn't want to have anything to do with them and didn't know who they were or where their office was. I didn't need their permission to be there so why did I need it to leave? Isn't that what the counselors and case managers are for? I never did make contact with someone in the medical department authorized to sign my form after trying three times.

I had to go to the R(eceiving) & D(ischarge) office at 9 AM that day with a box of what personal items I was taking home with me (i.e. pills, letters, books, photos, clothing, hygiene items) so they could be inspected and sealed. When I got there the employee told me to come back at Noon. Ok maybe he was busy with something else. I went back at noon and was told come back at 2:30. At 2:30 I was told to come back at 12:30 the next day. The next day that employee wasn't there. The one who was, "processed" me out and I was on my merry way. I was given about $90 cash as "travel money".

CHAPTER TWO

HALFWAY HOUSES

With my vacation at Club Fed at an end I was given a bus ticket and driven to a Greyhound bus station in Mobile, Alabama by another inmate. As I mentioned previously, the prison system has a job classification of "town driver" which is a position filled by an inmate who had a valid drivers' license before he was incarcerated. His duties are to shuttle inmates to a bus station, an airport or train station when they are released from the prison and headed to a halfway house. The drivers also take inmates to see real doctors if the BOP feels they are deserving of a second opinion or need anything beyond "basic" care. The on-call driver also ran errands for the camp such as refueling the vehicles and picking up materials at local retailers. The inmates whose time is up are not accompanied by any BOP employee. The time is considered a "furlough". It's part of the 30 such days over their visit. Don't hold your breath getting many of them. These "dangerous criminals" are loose in society. There was usually enough work for about 1 ½ drivers, but when I left the camp had four. The job paid about $100 a month but you had to deal with the staff and it was a job that I wanted no part of. One of my former bunkmates was the driver when I got to the camp and told me horror stories about botched appointments and scheduling. He was able to handle most of trips by himself so it was hard to imagine the need for four after he was released.

If you have family and are returning to the local area, they can come and pick you up if of course they have been approved and it's not likely you're about to disappear. You can also take a bus (which the BOP pays for) and then catch a taxi (also at BOP expense) when you get to your destination city. You can also fly at your own (your family's) expense. Both flying and family pickup have a limited window as to when you have to report to the halfway house. Bus trips take longer barring accidents, traffic and weather. I chose to take the bus (which was going to take 27 hours) because I wanted to make the BOP spend every dollar it had to on me since the cheap asses wouldn't give me my meds regularly. The bus ticket cost more than three and a half years of my $4 a month meds.

The more daring inmates schedule a bus trip and then have someone meet them at the bus station and go to the airport and fly. Seems the BOP never verifies anything. I guess they could have been charged with attempted escape or "being out of bounds" but some guys felt it worth the risk.

My family wanted to pick me up at the bus station in Youngstown, Ohio and take me out for a real meal before dropping me off at the halfway house. When my daughter called to "ask permission" she was told she could be charged with aiding an attempted escape. Dirtbags! Frankly the bus station and the halfway house are in an area I consider a "war zone" and no one should be there after dark anyway. My bus got in after dark on 12/6/11 so I took a taxi. Knowing the halfway house would confiscate any leftover cash I had I gave the taxi driver a big tip and wished him a merry Christmas. The halfway house was run by something called Community Corrections Association (CCA). My mother and daughter only came to visit during daylight hours.

When I checked in the first words out of the mouth of the attending staff employees were, "spread 'em, blow and give us a sample" NOT, where'd you come from? Have you been traveling long? Did you sleep? Do you need a shower? Did you eat anything? Do you need to call anyone? I just made a 27 hour whistle stop tour of the country and was stuck in Atlanta when I should have been sleeping. All my worldly possessions that I could carry (or were allowed to carry) were in a cardboard box about 2' high, 2' wide and 2' deep. I was wearing my sweatpants and sweatshirt, a winter coat and a set of thermal underwear. I didn't have a change of clothes, a towel, food or any money. None of which was offered to me.

My family called the facility three times over the next day or so to see if I had arrived safely and the person who answered the phone said they weren't allowed to give out that information. I was hoping my wife would make a Congressional complaint and then somebody would get their backside chewed up and be all apologetic. Since cell phones were verboten, I didn't have money for the pay phones, nor a calling card, so I couldn't call anyone. Finally about the third or fourth day one of the staff members allowed me to use the land line in the office and I called my daughter in Florida on their dime. I made a comment in front of the staff member sitting there that she should have called Washington and complained when they refused to acknowledge my being there.

The first time I stepped into the restroom/shower I was almost knocked over by the cigarette smoke. I thought I could get lung cancer without ever having smoked. The handbook I was given prior to arriving at this place said smoking was allowed but in designated areas. I didn't see a "smoking area" sign in the lavatory. The facility was going to be inspected sometime in January '12 so one of the residents went into the room with boots, disinfectant and a pressure washer and cleaned every wall, floor and fixture to get rid of the odor. Some guys just weren't satisfied that the staff called "smoke break" at least twice a day and took smokers outside to smoke. This was a big change from the Club Fed's no smoking policy.

Just as in the camp I was assigned a case manager. At the first meeting I had with him I made it clear I was supposed to be out of there in 14 days as per the Second Chance Act. He indicated the federal government wanted to get their inmates out as quickly as possible. I had to fill out a psych profile, which was a joke because they asked the same stupid questions in different ways, but was told I scored the lowest of anybody he'd ever tested. I guess if you don't smoke, drink, use drugs, molest children and know you didn't commit a crime you "pass".

Douglas P. Ro ile Sr.

One of the questions was, "what kind of help might you need now that you have been released from prison". My response was for help in writing a book exposing government idiocy, waste and corruption. I sure he didn't expect that and I didn't get help any. The staff also wanted me to sign a statement that I wouldn't sue Mahoning County (Ohio) if I were to be hurt on a job for the county. There was no reason for me to be assigned to any county work detail since I wasn't a state or county inmate or a local resident and I would have to have been brain dead to agree to something so ridiculous. I had to stand my ground and demand to speak to an attorney before they got the message. I resent being threatened. They gave up.

The psych profile was their way of deciding what additional "therapy" a resident needed before he could be released into society. I got stuck in two "classes" but made such a pain in the ass of myself I was excused from further attendance. One of the classes was about how to find a job. I was social security eligible and having been abused by the IRS, I wasn't going to work. The other class was for residents that had a substance abuse problem. (It seems the rocket scientists who design these programs labor under the erroneous assumption that everybody the government criminalized had to have an alcohol or drug problem). I made it very clear that I NEVER used drugs and was a political prisoner not a criminal. I didn't go to any more classes.

I'm fairly certain no one conducting the "classes" had a teaching certificate (in a union state), nor were they licensed psychologists or psychiatrists. So what were their qualifications? Where was their justification for trying to force me to attend?

After 10 days when it became apparent I was now a hostage at this facility, my mother and daughter brought me some money and an extra change of clothes and a towel. (One of the other residents had given me a towel a few days after I arrived so I could shower.) When they dropped off the items they asked a female staff member about my being able to leave for Christmas. The lady said no I hadn't been there long enough. I never asked them for anything after that. The money they gave me was in quarters but most of that was stolen from my unlocked clothes cabinet by one of the other residents.

The operators of this place were so heathen that they didn't even ask if anyone wanted to attend services on Christmas nor did they offer to provide transportation for such people. There was no local bus service on Christmas. I didn't get to attend mass on Christmas even though I attended regularly at the camp. To me it again re-enforces my choice for the title of this book.

To make my captivity even worse my case manager gave up his job and went back to being just another staff member. He never even started the paperwork to get me out of there on time. The new case manager told me I was his "guinea pig" and was going to work on my release right away. He told me these types of facilities were under pressure from the BOP to get guys out as quickly as possible. Allegedly his signature and a senior staff member was all that was needed before the paperwork went to a Mr. Armstrong in Cincinnati. Mr. Armstrong signed off on my released around middle of January but made it effective February 2nd. The extra time in February (31 hours to be exact) cost me $1,450 in social security benefits and the halfway house $360 in income.

The new case manager was in his late 20's and had a law degree from a school in New Hampshire. I told him what the world doesn't need is another lawyer. I think he wanted to concentrate on bankruptcy law. I voiced my displeasure with the entire operation of this facility on more than one occasion. He wanted me to fill out another stupid form about my time with them when I was finally leaving. One of the questions asked what I got from the experience. ABSOLUTELY NOTHING was my response, though that may not be entirely accurate. It was just another up close and personal experience of government idiocy and waste. The operator of the facility, Community Corrections Association, was being paid $2,000 a month by the federal Bureau of Prisons to house former inmates and help them find jobs. CCA confiscated 25% of a person's earnings for the privilege and claimed they had to give it to the BOP. The case manager had an interview for another job during the month I dealt with him. I sure hope he got it.

The only two aspects of my stay that I found acceptable was the fact that the quality of the food was better than FPC Pensacola, but the quantity wasn't, and I finally had access to a real computer and could communicate with my family and research business opportunities.

When I told one of the other staff members that I was finally leaving he suggested, "I bet your glad to be leaving this (expletive deleted) hole?" I said "can I quote you on that?" He said maybe I shouldn't.

I would have been better off staying 6 weeks in Pensacola because the weather in Ohio was cold. I was stuck inside the facility except when it was mealtime, or they graciously let us go job hunting or to the annex across the street to use the computers. It took almost a month before they let me know such was available. I told the first job placement director I didn't need a job and in an area with real unemployment at 15%, and I didn't feel right about taking a job from somebody who needed it. In a few months I was going back to Florida anyway. I told him that if I was forced to actually look for a job, when the question came up about why I wanted this job, I'd say "I don't", but I was threatened with being sent back to Club Fed if I didn't come here. I'm sure that wouldn't have impressed the person conducting the interview. Because my sole reason for being in a Youngstown, Ohio halfway house was to spend my home confinement time with my folks I would have had to quit any job I would have gotten in less than 3 months anyway. I didn't see that as being fair to the employer. I did have a former client who was willing to give me some work doing sorting and labeling but when I figured the cost of driving and paying into the Ponzi Scheme plus Ohio tax and the halfway house stealing 25% of the money I realized I'd be working for less than 50 cents on the dollar. I passed on the offer.

Sadly that employee was let go. He told me he was making only $25,000. I told him he was nuts, and that he had more talent than all that. His replacement was a veteran of the Coast Guard who bombed trying to run a restaurant. The one class I got stuck with about how to get a job was handled by him. I asked him point blank if he'd hire himself. I wouldn't hire him.

The low point of my stay was being threatened by a senior staff member over getting a job. I was told he didn't care how old I was, or where I was returning to, I was going to get a job or he'd pull me back in. A BOP employee overruled him. At one of the "team meetings" before I left Pensacola the Unit Manager suggested that most halfway houses had a requirement that get a job within 14 days or you risk being sent back from whence you came. I basically asked him which planet he was living on and wasn't he aware of the depression going on in the country. He didn't seem to care that I'd have an "income stream" (Social Security) once I got released, which is what the BOP really wants. Luckily his "tour of duty" was up a few months later and he retired. Good riddance, just another consummate pay-check stealing bureaucrat.

My pet peeve with this place was the numerous urine tests. First, there was NOTHING in my profile, background, or prior tests to suggest I ever smoked, drank or used drugs yet they loved harassing me with unnecessary tests. Seems nobody shares information or doesn't put any stock in prior tests. Second, even if it only cost $1 for the test it was a waste of money. I actually confronted the staff member who set up these allegedly "random" tests and asked him how much of a kickback he was getting for wasting money. Though he denied any such thing I think I made my point. The waste of money continued even after I was finally released to home confinement. When I voiced my objection (in writing) to Mr. Armstrong he told me he thinks all inmates are liars. Well Mr. Armstrong, I think all bureaucrats are overpaid and stealing their paychecks.

Because of the fact that I scored so low on the psych evaluation test I was able to avoid the "Allied" scourge. Allied Health Services was an organization that residents were FORCED to meet with to deal with whatever disorders their test score suggested they had in their life. It was just another program to collect government money and probably another no bid contract. Even though the administration didn't find it necessary to allow residents to attend services on Christmas or provide transportation for those that wanted to go, they "bent over backwards" to transport people to Allied appointments and make sure they were on time.

According to one of the guys I was friendly with who wasn't as fortunate as I was, said he met with a social worker, not a licensed clinical psychologist or a shrink. The sessions lasted about an hour and a half and some were twice a week. My friend thought they were a waste of time. I researched the ownership of both entities but didn't find any obviously commonality but being the cynic I am I'm dubious. I also looked for commonality with the company doing the urine testing. Nothing obvious showed up, but I'm still looking.

Almost as fast as I got to this place I was in the sights of one of the residents who was clearly "off the reservation". If he wasn't on meds he should have been and if he was supposed to be taking some he wasn't. He seemed fascinated with my every move even though I was making every attempt to ignore him, but finally he came out and threatened me. It seems he had threatened just about everybody else and at least one staff member. A short time later he went away cuffed and stuffed.

The halfway house facilities house former federal and state inmates. One side of this facility was for male residents and the other for females. The state inmates were allowed to have a cell phone, while federal ones were not. It was another case of bureaucratic idiocy and phones were rampant.

I was pleasantly surprised that contrary to what talk you hear in the camp I did not have to wear an ankle bracelet while on home confinement. I did walk around with a cordless phone in my pocket so the people at CCA could call me whenever they felt like it to make sure I hadn't run off. While it saved me money I still had to go back to the place twice a week for their useless and waste of money urine test. It was a 25 mile (one way) waste of gas. But hey, "It's all about the punishment".

I saw a certificate on the bulletin board that this facility had somehow been given an award for being a fine place. By whose standards? I wonder who they bribed for it.

CHAPTER THREE

IS THIS JUSTICE?

Even though "we're tough of crime", the harsh reality of life is that costs set in. The government rocket scientists spent over $100,000 on me alone. There is a lot of talk and writings these days about budgets and overcrowding in both federal and state prisons, the abuses of private prisons and the costs associated with elderly inmates. Sadly too much of it is just that, talk. The two million plus people who are incarcerated can't vote, donate to a campaigns, may not have family and are portrayed as evil in society, so they don't count. Somebody needs to remind bureaucrats of the scripture passage about ".. what you do to the least of my brethren..". (Matt. 25:40)

Bernard Kerik, a former NY City Police Commissioner, who pleaded guilty in 2009 to eight counts, including tax evasion and lying to the White House spent four years as a guest of the federal government. He has since stated, "If the American people and members of Congress saw what I saw, there would be anger, there would be outrage, and there would be change, because nobody would stand for it." They say prison changes a person. I wonder what he was thinking when he was "locking them up and throwing away the key." He had been nominated to head of the Department of Homeland Security but withdrew his name as a nominee when he admitted hiring an illegal immigrant. He now appears to be an advocate for prison reform and is a contributor on FOX News.

There is a simple solution to prison reform, stop putting PEOPLE in prison and start putting CRIMINALS in prison, unless of course your name is Clinton. I saw so many petty, trivial, justify my job situations even worse than my own at FPC Pensacola. I was so disgusted it motivated me add this section to the book. Until it happens to your family no one knows how corrupt the legal system is or what a farce the low level prison system is, and Hilary got pass from them. Based on what idiocy I saw and lived through she should be doing "life without".

Of the guys on my first work detail four were white collar "offenders" and two were drug offenders. Their sentences ranged from thirteen months to eight years. None of the white collar guys should have been in prison and the drug guys had abusive sentences. It's long past time to stop sentencing anybody to jail, prison, halfway houses, work camps etc. for first time non-violent occurrences. I know Bernie Madoff was a 1st time offender. His alleged $60 billion scam is now down to approved claims of about $17.5 billion. The latest news out is that the trustee has recovered about ten billion dollars for his victims. Is the system going to modify his sentence? When the government wastes at least 25% ($2.5 billion) a day with complete lack of accountability how can you send anybody to prison for 150 years for $7.5 billion?

The government runs the biggest Ponzi scheme in history (Social Security), so why aren't all former and present Congressmen/women and Senators in jail for a term similar to Madoff's? Oh I forgot: bureaucrats and politicians think they are above the law. Or is it because the government thinks it can print its way out of any Social Security "crisis" until the dollar collapses?

If we eliminated the income tax system, legalized drugs and had immigration reform Congress could shut down a lot of federal and state prisons, layoff dozens of prosecutors and a maybe a third of the federal judges and related underlings. Taxpayers could get a raise through lower taxes. The U.S. government is staffed with hypocrites when it comes to talking about "human rights violations" to other countries when we have the highest prison population in the world solely to make money and create jobs for unionized paycheck stealing bureaucrats. (Some of prison staff at Pensacola didn't belong to the union because they aren't allowed to strike). If prison life is the deterrent the experts claim why are we not building more prisons? The problem with building prisons is that you have to put people in them to justify them, and then you have to pay for them. The "tough on crime" mentality comes with a price. Once politicians stop making criminals out of people a bunch of paycheck stealing bureaucrats are going to be out of a job.

After watching the latest two appointments to the U.S. Supreme Court I wonder why we need the federal court system at all. The "Supremes" cherry pick the cases they feel are worthy of their time, and issue convoluted decisions. Bush vs. Gore, ObamaCare, Roe vs. Wade, gay marriage, the 15% good behavior nonsense and a case involving honest services of elected officials are just a few of the many decisions I disagree with. These decisions support the government and not the people. They don't seem to place much stock in their oath of office about protecting us "... against all enemies foreign and domestic" primarily the domestic ones.

How can anyone respect judges who don't believe God's law trumps man's law, ("...neither are your ways my ways......so are my ways higher than your ways...")[23], who condone pornography as free speech, abortion as choice, spit on your right to bear arms, steal your property for a shopping center, refuse to use DNA evidence, abets a terrorist organization (the IRS), and willfully drags out the whole legal process even though the people lose at a percentage somewhat near body temperature? I am now a strong advocate for abolishing what is affectionately known as the Department of "Justice". The latest Clinton "white-wash" is the icing on the cake. Injustice is probably more accurate if you've ever been attacked by it. They obviously refuse to enforce EXISTING immigration laws, yet I went to prison for exercising my right to free speech.

---

[23]   Isiah chapter 55 v. 8-9

Most of the "Supremes" work is done by clerks, and they're only in session for nine months (excluding holidays and weekends). Americans should be demanding that all levels of government write PLAIN ENGLISH, clear and concise laws? According to the Supreme Court decisions going back decades (1926, Connally vs General Construction), "where the law is uncertain and vague, there is no law". Why shouldn't all decisions handed down by the "Supremes" have to be 6-3 to be binding?

I posed this question to several of lawyers who were guests of the government with me: "What crime HAS TO BE a federal crime, without saying treason" (which should be handled by the military). Not one of them could give me one. Before someone says "tax crimes" I suggest you re-read the first part of this book. Once the income tax is gone even that won't fly. I wonder how many billions we could save once we could eliminate a lot of the DOJ lawyers, a whole bunch of judges, shut down more than half the federal prisons, layoff a bunch of the BOP employees and eliminate the related pensions and health care costs?. Many of the alleged offenses people in this country are persecuted for (yes I said PERsecuted) aren't even crimes in other countries.

One of the other "guests" with me at Club Fed wasn't an American citizen but was attacked under an obscure provision of the "Turn America into a Police State Act" (aka The Patriot Act) because his employer did business in the U.S. He was charged with involvement in a price fixing scheme. The "crime" was so heinous he spent seven months with us. ABSOLUTE NONSENSE. The alleged actions that our Department of Injustice criminalized, weren't illegal in his own country. Sadly his employer terminated him, though I think he had a great case for unlawful discharge. He spent about $400,000 on legal fees and lost on a technicality. Trust me America wasn't any safer because the government attacked this man.

Sadly it isn't a "justice" system any longer, just a totally broken "legal system". I could write a thousand pages about what judicial "activism" but the subject is covered quite well in *"Betrayed by the Bench, How*

Judge-made Law Has Transformed America's Constitution, Courts and Culture"[24] by John Stormer and *"Lies the Government Told You"* [25]by Andrew Napolitano. It should open your eyes and make you sick. From my perspective, one innocent person incarcerated is much worse than 99 guilty ones who may have gotten away. The innocent one was probably the victim of shoddy work by law enforcement, which may also be the reason the other 99 didn't get arrested/convicted.

Though the 6th amendment to the Constitution GUARANTEES you the right to "trial by jury" for any matter over $20, try to get one in a civil case in the federal legal system. Been there done that! It is a wanton disregard of the Constitution based on nonsense that your right to a trial by jury might clog up the court system. Here's the solution, STOP TERRORIZING people. You're supposed to put criminals (i.e. pay check stealing bureaucrats, bureaucrats who grossly mismanagement public money, those who ignore the constitution) in jail not people. You might even throw in a few murders, rapists, kidnappers, child molesters and those who abuses the elderly occasionally. None of which needs to be a federal crime.

In my life the only decision that the Supreme Court ever made that I strongly agreed with was "Miranda vs. Arizona", yet activist judges have slowly chipped away at that. That decision came out about a year after I was hassled, as a teenager, by the local police while trying to do "the right thing" (report/return finding stolen property). Before it was all done two of my friends and I were being accused of stealing. We were picked up from work, never allowed a phone call or given our "rights". At the time it was all perfectly legal. In this day and age every high school senior today should be lectured about the Fifth Amendment, "...you have the right to remain silent", (USE IT) before they get a diploma. Hilary's people sure are aware of it and exercised it. To this day I have nothing but contempt for cops and very little respect for lawyers and judges who are part of the criminal justice system. Like most Americans I live in fear of them,

---

[24]   John Stormer, 2005, Liberty Bell Press

[25]   Andrew Napolitano, 2010, Thomas Nelson

(though I do not condone violence) which isn't how "free" people in a "civilized" society are suppose too live.

The purpose of the federal appeals courts is also highly suspect. They turn down 95+% of all cases that come before them. What good is a process that supports the suppression of evidence, rigged juries, prosecutor misconduct, perjury, intimidation of witnesses and abandons any search for the truth? How could the country or the people be any worse off with just a state court system? Luckily most of those judges are elected by the people not appointed by which ever lesser of two evils we let into the White House, and the voters do have a way to get rid of them. The people who started the "Jail for Judges" website have a fan in me.

The Chief Justice of the 9th Circuit Court of Appeals in a ruling in the Milke case said, "No civilized system of justice should have to depend on such flimsy evidence, quite possibly tainted by dishonesty or overzealousness, to decide whether to take someone's life or liberty". In the prologue I asked, are we a civilized society? I'm not sure we are.

In May of 2011 "60 Minutes" did a story on a man named Tom Drake who was charged with violating the Espionage Act for blowing the whistle on "Project Trailblazer". It was an alleged "classified" project (BTW: everything in Washington seems to be "national security/classified" because they have to hide the truth and their incompetency from us) that was a $1.25 billion waste of money. A similar project known as "Thin-thread" would have only cost $3 million, that's million with an "M". The National Security Agency director was obviously an idiot and again nobody was accountable. Being a whistle blower is OK as long as you don't expose government idiocy and waste.

Homicide is probably the most heinous crime anyone can commit, with rape, child abuse and kidnapping not far behind. A violent offender can only be executed once no matter how many people they kill, yet even though every state has laws against homicide the feds had to get into the act with a FEDERAL law of "depriving someone of their civil rights" (i.e. killing them) even though dead is dead. If the feds think it's a "hate crime" they want to prosecute it. Is that going to bring the deceased back to life? What difference is there who executes them? Dead is dead! But hey, we're tough on crime!

When a gun is involved we hear the typical uproar about taking away guns.

FACT: When guns are outlawed, outlaws will have guns.

FACT: Guns don't kill people, people kill people. (Why don't we ban cars, baseball bats, knives, scissors, screwdrivers and Schedule 3 prescription drugs among other things that kill).

FACT: The BEST defense against a bad guy with a gun is a good guy with a gun.

The Sandy Hook gunman committed four crimes before killing one person at the school. (Theft of his mother's gun, murder of his mother, entering a school area with a loaded firearm, and breaking and entering.) My question is why didn't an alarm that would have awaken the dead go off the moment the building was breached? A good guess was they didn't think mayhem could happen in their town. So their error in judgment means the federal government AGAIN clamors about gun control. I have never owned a gun, shot a gun and now that I'm a "felon" will probably never own one but I know we have plenty of gun laws. Three other guests of the government with me were in prison over the most petty gun law violations I'd ever heard of and one of them was former military who served honorably. BUT WE'RE TOUGH ON CRIME. Anybody remember "Fast & Furious"?

The USA and Russia are the top two arms dealers in the world and they have no idea where many of those weapons may end up.

Another waste is that the FEDS want to get involved in every incident where drugs are found or involved. It's not bad enough that ANYONE found in possession of drugs is immediately thought of as a "trafficker" and if a state line is crossed the Feds seize control of the case.

"The ineffective war on drugs initiated by the Nixon (R) administration (the only president who was forced to resign) has lasted forty-two years, cost $2.5 Trillion dollars resulting in 45 million arrests, and America is no closer to being drug free and WILL NEVER BE drug free." [26] It's long past time to shut down prisons and jails, layoff judges and prosecutors, repair families and legalize drugs. Drug trafficking exists solely because of profit. Take the profit out and it will eliminate lots of violent crimes. The government will actually collect tax dollars not waste them. We can downsize the Department of Injustice. The Treasury/Congress wants additional revenue well here's a great source.

Prohibition did not work with alcohol in the "Roaring 20's" and the entire war in drugs is a dismal failure. I would suggest that in order to help with rising health care costs that anyone purchasing these controlled substances (once they are legal) be forced to sign a statement that they will not be treated at taxpayer expense for any condition attributable to such use. That probably would cover just about anything they need treatment for. It is way past time to start instilling personal responsibility and constantly preach about the consequences of drug usage. The country doesn't need to coddle people who willingly engage in self-destructive behavior. I would also establish a similar ban on medical treatment to illnesses brought about by alcohol and cigarette abuse.

One of the guys in the room I was first assigned to had thirty year sentence involving marijuana because he wouldn't cooperate with the government. Another inmate got thirty years because he had money but no drugs.

The scariest part of the federal court system is that the judges <u>never</u> leave. I give you Supreme Court Justice Ginsburg. Now that Trump has won she'll hang on until her last breath to deny him the chance to put

---

[26] FED-Cure, prison reform organization

another conservative on the court. There is no mandatory retirement age. They become power freaks and won't just fade off into the sunset. When pondering retirement Supreme Court Justices usually are worried about upsetting the balance of power on the court. In 2014 it was four conservatives, four liberals and one "swing" vote. With the death of Judge Scalia in 2016 the fight began over who would appoint his replacement and sway the balance of power. While they may see themselves as brilliant jurists nobody deserves a lifetime appointment and ninety percent of their salary as a pension. Can you imagine "rewarding" anybody who votes to steal your freedom, your liberty, and spits on the Constitution?

The gross mismanagement of public money should be #1 crime on the list of non-violent offenses. Non-violent crimes are commercial crimes because they involve money. Rather than being obsessed with throwing people in jail and beating our chests about being "tough on crime" why don't we make "violators" pay their "debt to society" thru restitution and REAL community service? I wonder if Bernie Madoff's victims would rather have him in prison or have their money back? I think that's a no-brainer, but then some promotion seeking, headline grabbing, governor-wannabe prosecutor wouldn't be able to get his 15 minutes of fame. The man's life expectancy may be 15 years even with access to competent medical treatment, so why a 150 year sentence? To show "we're tough on crime"? Twenty years would have been a death sentence. As I said previously the medical treatment in the federal prison system is tantamount to attempted murder anyway so I wouldn't bet on the 15 years, though if God has a sense of humor maybe he'll keep Bernie around long enough to be a burden to the system. About 40 more years would be good. Every regulator who allegedly investigated this company should be sharing a cell with him for dereliction of duty.

The government continues to allege there are 11 million illegal immigrants in this country who obviously broke and are continuing to break the law. Are they working? As Contract Labor? Under the table/ off the books? Are they filing income tax returns? Are they going to file? How are they going to pay? If so how did they get a social security number? If not why are we giving them amnesty? The ironic part is they may qualify for the "poverty credit" and be able to get free social security credits, unemployment and health care if they were legal. Part of Mr. Snipes' sentence was one year even though he didn't owe a dime in taxes for one particular year and he's a legal citizen. The judge didn't show any consideration for that. FILING was the only issue. Since the government can't (and isn't going to) put 11 million people in prison or deport them, and the illegals know it, why incarcerate any non-violent 1st time offender? The government puts out statistics that suggest they deport maybe 3% of the illegals each year. My question is how many of them sneak back in? Multiple times?

QUERY: Is the legal system "selectively" enforcing the law or whatever law they choose this week? Is "prosecutorial discretion" out of control? Obviously, and The Clintons are proof of it. Eleven million is a lot of votes. I wonder how the government can be certain of the number when they can't even get the census accurate. Every 10 years some state or minority group is complaining about an undercount.

Sadly the process is no longer about "tough on crime" or justice. With the passage of the "Turn America into a Police State Act" everyone living in this country is considered a terrorist. It's about controlling every aspect of our lives. What we do, what we say, think, read and need. It's also about keeping the system alive and employing bureaucrats who are dirtbags, liars and power freaks. Once they get drunk on power and know there is no accountability they do whatever they want. Luckily the day will come when they all will meet the ultimate judge who'll sort them out and remind them about "….. what you did to the least of my brethren….." Unfortunately not soon enough for most of the two million plus people now incarcerated.

In my opinion, the 2000 presidential election debacle in Florida was one of the four all-time low points for the Supreme Court. Roe vs. Wade, Obama-care and gay marriage were the others. While there have been countless convoluted, ridiculous, basis-less decisions, "selecting" the president of the United States ranks at the top of the activism meter. The decisions on Obama-care and gay marriages just about puts the nail in the coffin. A woman who didn't want pay to estate taxes was used as a path to overturn the Defense of Marriage Act signed by a President whose own marriage is a joke. Where was the "soak the rich" crowd when she wanted special treatment?

To suggest that the operation of the federal courts today was in keeping with the intent of the founding fathers is laughable. No function of the federal government today was what the founders envisioned. They believed in a weak central government and STATES rights and PEOPLE's rights. That's why the 10th Amendment is an integral part of the Bill of Rights. Now about the only right the people have left is to shut up and pay the protection money. Even worse, if you don't know your rights, you don't have any rights. The founders also believed in God and said so. The present day jurists don't want any mention of God (school prayer, pledge of allegiance, Ten Commandments) yet they protect "gay" rights and the murder of unborn children. How can a court with six members who claim to be Roman Catholic allow such practices to exist? Fact: GOD'S LAW TRUMPS MAN'S LAW and if you don't believe that or agree with that LEAVE.

Americans need to demand a system of "people's courts" where a search for the truth is paramount and rules of procedures are thrown in the garbage. The country needs a system where judges, bureaucrats and politicians can be accountable to their employers, the American people; a system in which you get your day in court quickly; a system where lawyers are considered accessories to the former abuses of the old system, and delays, continuances and stall tactics are forbidden. Jury duty should be mandatory for every adult. Jurors should be allowed to question witnesses and made aware of their right to nullify the law.[27] Only in the case of violent crime (murder, rape, kidnapping, armed robbery, espionage, obvious acts of terrorism by NON-US citizens and treason)

---

[27]   U.S. v Moylan, 1969, 4th Circuit affirmed jury nullification

should a state or military court get involved, but with jurors having the same rights.

"Perhaps one of the most unconscionable acts of greed by government is the confiscating a person's home in order to transfer it to other people, who are expected to build things that will pay more taxes." [28](Thomas Sowell)

How about this: FBI two years behind on computer system. The project is $100 million over budget and only half finished.[29] Did anybody get fired? Demoted? Prosecuted? Go to jail? The "justice" department lost real taxpayer dollars. I got punished for imaginary dollars.

Former Congressman Jim Traficant on the pursuit of Roger Clemens: "Once again, the Justice Department continues to seek out high profile Americans for the sake of headlines, NOT Justice. Thousands of families are being destroyed due to the over-zealous investigations, often criminal, to pacify the egos of Government misfits". (I couldn't have said it better). Further he goes on "Congress lies to the American people on a regular basis". "There were thousands of tobacco industry executives who told Congress, under oath, that "tobacco is not harmful to anyone's health". Are any of those so-called experts in prison for lying? If it was appropriate for Martha Stewart why not them?

Making criminals out of as many people as possible is an indirect way of taking away their right to vote and own a gun. Neither of which is otherwise popular.

A FEW RELATED QUOTES:

"We put small thieves in prison and elect big thieves to public office". (Neal Boortz, 8/25/11).

---

[28] *Uncle Sam's greedy*, Thomas Sowell, Oct. 15, 2010 Youngstown Vindicator
[29] USA Today, Kevin Johnson, Oct. 21, 2010

You cannot legislate morality (Drugs, porn, alcohol abuse, abortion etc.)

I get $75K a year to not work", a maintenance supervisor at FPC Pensacola to an inmate.

Sadly, the Constitution guarantees free speech, it doesn't guarantee listeners.

CHAPTER FOUR

SOLUTIONS

While there are lobbying efforts to "reform" the criminal "justice" system and the federal prison system the facts are, there are only about 220,000 people in federal prisons spread out over 50 states. The Department of (In)Justice's budget is about $8 billion. That's less than one half of one percent of the annual federal budget. It is LOW priority item for Congress. Even with two Afro-American Attorneys General nothing was happening. In the case of Mr. Holder he should be in prison over "Fast & Furious". While it may be the function of underlings in Washington to give the boss, "plausible deniability" the fish stinks from the head first. Some of my fellow inmates were in prison for what they "should have known" because of the job/position they held. Again, a double standard for elected officials and bureaucrats vs. ordinary Americans.

Even if all the inmates' families took an active role in trying to effect change they don't usually vote, aren't a large enough voting-block, and they don't make significant donations to campaigns. There are two lobbying groups, FedCure and Families Against Mandatory Minimums (FAMM) that try to help inmates and their families, but they are beating they're heads against a brick wall. One of the lawyer/inmates suggested to me, when the BOP wastes taxpayer money arguing in the Supreme Court to deprive inmates of 7 extra days/year of good behavior time you know they aren't serious about prison reform. Only when "We the People" get serious about "throwing the bums out" and holding those that were evicted accountable and sent to prison, will REAL prison reform happen.

The most obvious solution to overcrowded prisons and real spending cuts is to have a balanced budget amendment. Such an amendment which will eventually lead to hard choices, one of which will recognize shutting down all Federal Prison Camps and low security facilities is a must. If society has been "injured" by non-violent, first-time, low level offenders, let the people who need punished perform real community service. Fines or some monetary punishment could also be imposed assuming of course any of them could get a job with a criminal history on their resume.

The Bureau of Prison's "mission statement" says "…to protect society by confining….." Protect society from what? Frankly, the social costs associated with incarceration of first time, non-violent offenses can't be justified. If eighty percent of marriages of incarcerated inmates end in divorce the dirtbags, liars and power freaks are only adding to the welfare rolls. Let's see, the government:

a) Isn't collecting taxes, b) is paying to take care of the inmate, c) is paying to take care of the family, and d) got stuck paying off mortgages when the homes of inmates went into foreclosure. That "tough on crime" nonsense has to change.

Number two in accomplishing prison reform is to abolish the Sentencing Commission and reducing drastically the number of "federal" crimes. If politicians keep looking for reasons to put people in jail I'm sure they'll find one or invent one. "*Three felonies a day, How the Feds Target the Innocent*"[30] is a book that is a must read and should shock everyone. Let Congress set the parameters for punishing what few crimes actually have to be federal crimes, after all too many members of Congress were prosecutors and lawyers, and they have that "tough on crime mentality."

---

[30]   Harvey Silvergate, 2011

While many inmates are chomping at the bit to get to halfway houses they are a bigger waste of time than the camps and also need to be abolished. Inmates who will eventually be released should be "close to home", should have access to local job placement services and furloughs to pursue them. The DOJ has the technology to electronically keep track of those on probation and if Congress truly wanted former inmates to "re-integrate into society" they would expunge all first time non-violent offenses from the record once an "offender" has "paid his debt to society".

Inmates on home confinement are forced to return to the halfway houses for needless/wasteful urine tests sometimes having to travel two hours.

As part of the Second Chance Act of 2007, a "pilot" program was set up to "test market" releasing inmates over 65 who had already served 75% of a sentence of 10 years or more. (The ones the Bureau of Prisons admit cost them the most money) A whopping 71 inmates across the country were released before January 2012. Only four left Pensacola and it was two years <u>after</u> the law was signed. Every one of those inmates got a dose of bureaucratic runaround first and the process just another example of lip service over substance. Can you say "fear of losing my job".

Ronald Fraser, a public policy writer for the Washington-based DKT Liberty Project, had a column entitled *Smart way to cut prison cost* in July, 2011. It appeared in the Warren Tribune Chronicle on July 5th. Mr. Fraser suggested a four part solution:

a)   Increase the early release credit (Make 15% mean 15%),
b)   Keep non-violent first time offenders out of prison,
c)   Probation NOT jail,
d)   Nix mandatory minimums.

All of these are long overdue.

The age old question is should we be spending taxpayer money on prisons or education, prisons or medical care, prisons or child nutrition, prisons or private sector job programs assuming the government had the money in the first place. Obviously the war on drugs is a dismal failure. The TSA had never caught one terrorist. One quarter of the population doesn't file a tax return, and even when one is filed the government can't always collect. Yet the gross mismanagement of public money and the abuse of power goes on daily and politicians are worried about looking soft on crime.

The Hilary Clinton national security/server fiasco was the crown jewel that supports the title of this book. She was guilty as hell and the Department of Injustice did not have the guts to enforce the law. Even worse FBI employees were forced to sign confidentiality statements to basically suppress the truth. She is the ultimate liar and power freak, her husband the ultimate dirtbag.

WAKE UP AMERICA

Part Three
POLITICIANS

CHAPTER ONE

"LIES, DAMN LIES AND STATISTICS"

"There are three kinds of lies: "Lies, Damn Lies and Statistics", words attributed to Mark Twain, about people trying to make a point or win an argument. Politicians come to mind.

According to its definition, a large gathering of almost any species can be called a "congress". A Wikipedia post tried to suggest it applied specifically to baboons. That may be an insult to baboons, but may explain why Washington is so dysfunctional.

FACT: Politicians and diapers should be changed quite often for the very same reason.

It has been said, "Insanity is doing the same thing over and over and expecting a different result." So why do we keep sending the same dirtbags, liars and power freaks back to Washington? People can't influence a political party to do the right thing if you stick with it when it does the wrong thing.

Ben Stein (commentator and speechwriter) gave a new definition of insanity: It seems under Obamacare you have to prove you have health insurance but you don't have to prove you're a citizen.

Edward Langley had a great quote, "What this country needs is more unemployed politicians" to which I will add "and paycheck stealing bureaucrats".

Nearly all men can stand adversity, but if you want to test a man's character, give him power! (Abraham Lincoln)

Bob Woodward, of the Washington Post, (2013) said "...a rat's nest of concealment and lies is at the heart of many of the Obama administration scandals and miscues".

The greatest lie ever told is "I'm from the government and I'm here to help you".

Will Rogers, (cowboy, humorist and actor from the 1920's and '30's) had a great line, "...be very afraid Congress is in session. "I think that's even better advice today with the "Patriot" Act and ObamaCare being the crowns jewel of idiocy.

Those are some profound statements that support my hypothesis, and most Americans could agree with, however lip service isn't enough. Washington, DC is the most corrupt city in the United States and is certainly the modern day Sodom and Gomorra. It is infested with dirtbags, liars and power freaks and we certainly need to "clean out the swamp" as Princess Nancy (Pelosi) called it (echoed by Donald Trump) starting with her.

Princess Nancy keeps her job as a party leader because she raises a great deal of money for other Democratic candidates, (all of which are outside her district, and she can't vote in any of those districts). She reminds fellow liberal D's of that fact when it comes time to vote on legislation she wants pushed forward.

I had hoped the "Tea Party Revolution" of 2010 was the start of a real change of attitude in that regard. After the 2008 elections I felt it would be a "cold day in hell" before any Republican could get elected dog catcher, let alone President, for many years to come. But in 2010, the Democrats managed to snatch defeat from the "jaws of victory".

Politicians the voters keep sending back to Washington have long since abandoned the idea that they public servants. The vast majority of them don't have their constituents' or America's best interest at heart. The voters have abdicated their role as Masters and become slaves in exchange for handouts and free stuff. During his presidential campaign in 1992, Ross Perot suggested that too many people go to Washington to cash-in not to serve, and the ones with good intentions get corrupted by the system. Some senators that get/got disgusted and after one term, actually do/did the honorable thing, they retire.

I believe NO LAW is much better than BAD LAW, and America has plenty of bad laws. It's a shame Congress doesn't devote one entire session for repealing bad, outdated, vague and abusive laws, before they pass any new ones. Obamacare would be a nice place to start.

Former Orlando Sentinel journalist Charlie Reese's column titled "545 People" appeared on the internet in 2013. It first appeared in Mr. Reese's column in 1985 and as his final column in 2001. If you haven't seen it, here's some excerpts of it: (Words in parentheses are mine)

"Politicians are the only people in the world who CREATE problems and then campaign against them. All the (Republi-crats) rail against deficits but yet we still have deficits. They give lip service to being against high taxes and yet we have high taxes. The taxpayers don't propose a budget that spends more than we take in, the President does. The president doesn't spend a dime, Congress does. (President Reagan made this point often, yet was blamed for the national debt rising from $1 trillion to $3.2 trillion over his eight year term. Bill Clinton added $1.6 trillion which was more than everybody before Reagan, and yet he was elected twice and is worshipped by the Democrats). While the President can propose a budget, he cannot force Congress to accept it. The taxpayers never get a vote in fiscal policy, appropriations or monetary policy."

"One Hundred Senators, 435 Congressmen/women, one President and nine Supreme Court Justices equates to 545 human beings out of 310+ million people who are directly, legally, morally and individually responsible for the domestic problems that plague the country." (Mr. Reese excluded members of the Federal Reserve Board, a problem was created by Congress). "Congress delegated its constitutional duty to provide a sound currency to a federally chartered, but private, central bank."

Mr. Reese goes on, "it seems inconceivable to me that a nation of 300 million cannot replace 545 people who stand convicted, by the present facts, of incompetence and irresponsibility. I can't think of a single domestic problem that is not traceable directly to those 545 people. When you fully grasp the plain truth that 545 people exercise the power of the federal government, then it must follow, that what exists is what they want to exist."

"If the tax code is unfair, it's because they want it unfair. If the budget is in the red, it's because they want it in the red. If the army and marines are in Iraq, it's because they want them in Iraq. If they do not receive social security but are on an elite retirement plan not available to the people, it's because they want it that way."

"There is no insoluble government problem. Do not let these 545 people shift the blame to bureaucrats, whom they hire and whose jobs they can abolish; to lobbyists, whose gifts and bribes they can reject; to regulators, to whom they give the power to regulate and from whom they can take this power. Above all, do not let them con you into the belief that there exist disembodied mystical forces like the economy, inflation, or politics that prevent them from doing what they took an oath to do"

"These 545 people and they alone are responsible. They alone have the power. They and they alone should be held accountable by the people who are the bosses, provided the voters have the gumption to manage their own employees. We should vote all of them out of office and clean up their mess".

It's long past time to Wake Up America. It's time to send them all packing. "Throw Them All Out, How politicians and their friends get rich off insider stock ties, land deals, and cronyism that would send the rest of us to jail" is the previously mentioned book by Peter Sweitzer, after the insider trading habits of Congress-critters became public.

The members of Congress elected by the Tea Party in the 2010 midterms have not been in office long enough for me to fairly criticize, but even they need to be term limited. I was hoping the voters would get the message and continue the momentum of 2010, however the 2012, 2014and 2016 elections show there is still a lot of work to be done.

Elected officials are never going to change as long as American voters give credibility to the notion that they are stupid (Jonathan Gruber revelations, 2014, ObamaCare)[31] and incapable of governing themselves. If reducing crime involves preventing repeat offenders, the voters can start by not re-electing them. As Mr. Perot suggested, too many of them are there to cash in, not serve, and want to avail themselves of the generous benefits they approved.

I once heard it said that if a person wasn't a Democrat by the time they're 20 they have no heart, but if they're not a Republican by the time they're 40 they have no brains. I want to add an addendum that says if you're not Libertarian long before 50 there's no hope for you. Maybe your right to vote should be rescinded. (As a side note the Libertarian Party BLEWWWWWWWWW a golden opportunity to elect a President in 2016 since neither Trump nor Clinton was popular, but they couldn't get behind the right person).

---

[31]   Examiner.com, Nov. 10, 2014, *Obamacare architect admits Obama lied about his signature law*, Jim Kouri

Winston Churchill, a former prime minister of England, said America <u>will</u> ultimately do the right thing, AFTER they tried everything else. Clint Eastwood suggested that the world views Americans as dumbasses. In November of 2012 they went to the polls and proved them right!

One of the most blatant government lies is the unemployment rate. How can any number that doesn't count people who gave up looking for a job be any indicator of unemployment? What about those that are working well below their education and experience levels? And those who have to have two day jobs and a weekend job just to put food on the table? But dirtbags, liars and power freaks love to brag about the unemployment rate going down especially when they manipulate the numbers. My question is if all the jobs that were lost under Obama have now been recovered[32] are they: a) the same job, b) with the same pay, c) in the same location, and d) with the same benefits, or are they just statistics to grab headlines? I vote for statistics.

Valerie Jarrett, an Obama senior adviser (that's the job title they give to their cronies to create a job for them) suggested that unemployment payments stimulates the economy. Let's see, the government steals from those willing to work, and from businesses that could have been given the money to its employees, to give it to those who are unwilling to work or will milk the system for free stuff until they are forced to go back to work. Wouldn't allowing the people the government stole from to keep and spend their money themselves stimulate the economy? Hypocrisy at its finest

---

[32]   CNNMoney, *U.S. soon to recover all the jobs lost in the financial crisis*; Annalyn Kurtz, June, 2014

CHAPTER TWO

WHO'S TO BLAME

For all those Americans who have come to believe the idea that "they're all crooks, but he's (she) our crook", here's the record of the "Republi-crats":

1) The true national debt is well over $130 trillion, not the almost nineteen+ trillion published amount. The $19+ trillion does not include any of the obligations taxpayers have for all the future pensions, medical costs of every person who ever worked for the federal government, served in the military or is a senior citizen. Ex-military men and women wounded "fighting for their country" are going to need a lot of care. For every person drawing a paycheck from the government there is one person who used to have the job collecting a taxpayer subsidized pension and medical treatment. Those costs could be more than the salary they received for screwing up the country and making financial slaves of all of us. It is the largest unfunded liability in existence yet is never mentioned when the national debt is discussed. No one knows how large it is or will be because life expectancy and medical costs go up every year. Such liabilities speak to the long term viability of any entity, business etc. Sadly too many of the government miscreants were stealing their paycheck and have a union protecting them. Failure to adequately disclose such liabilities by publicly traded companies will get an auditor or CEO at least fired, or thrown in jail because it taints the true

financial condition of the company. Taxpayers are also on the hook for all the mortgages, loans and foreign aid the government has promised. That's through the SBA, Freddie Mac, FNMA, Sally Mae and dozens of treaties. The wars in Middle East aren't even part of those numbers.

2) Passed the "Turn America In to a Police State Act" in 2001, affectionately known as the Patriot Act. They literally spit on the Constitution even though they love to give lip service to standing up for the rule of law. This law stole the rights to privacy, free speech and due process of all Americans in the name of security and safety. In 1755, Benjamin Franklin made the statement "Those who surrender freedom for security will not have, nor do they deserve, either one". The American people should declare a national day of mourning for the passage of this travesty.

3) Turned America into an entitlement state based on socialistic ideas. Fifty percent of the population pays little or no federal income tax, yet demand free everything as though the Constitution guaranteed it. These people have access to the interstate highways, government schools, the fire department, the police department, national parks, free food and medical care? The most abused words in the US Constitution are "...to promote the general welfare..." They're found in the preamble, not the actual Constitution, yet have been used to justify making America a society of moochers. How is it "promoting the general welfare" to allow unmarried women to give birth to multiple children with multiple partners and then suggest somebody (i.e. government/taxpayers) has to pay for those children? I'll give them a pass for the first time they got pregnant (young, dumb, drunk, high, raped), but what's your excuse for the 2nd, 3rd, 4th etc. time?

4) Think creating jobs means padding the government payroll by creating agencies that hire useless, overpaid, unionized, paycheck

stealing bureaucrats who create nothing but aggravation. These people expect a pension and health care for life for having been a "loyal government employee" even though they ruined the country. The union that represents the IRS workers is doing its best to keep the present system because they'd suffer a loss of power and membership. Bureaucrats deliver no product or service, yet they have driven billions in wealth outside the United States with taxes and regulations that are crippling small business. Every small business hopes to be a big business someday but the Obama administration seemed to despise capitalism. Socialism and communism are both failures where ever they were tried.

5) Have lost the will to declare war. With all of our alleged "intelligence gathering" we have no idea who or where the enemy is. America presently occupies 130 countries with over 800 bases. Way too much money is unaccounted for or wasted. Our troops don't have proper gear, protection, equipment and some wonder what they got themselves into, and are neglected if and when they come home.

6) Have destroyed the education system in this country. The "dumbing down of America" if you will. People who want their kids to learn (the truth) send them to private schools or home school them and avoid government schools like the plague. Common Core and No Child Left Behind were not the answer.

7) Condone efforts to avoid any reference to God, even though George Washington said, "when we fail to be one nation UNDER GOD, we become a nation gone under." Politicians can't figure out how to justify taking "In God we Trust" off of Federal Reserve Notes so they're moving America closer to a cashless society.

8) Watch Medicare waste $60 billion a year thru fraud and poor management. Medicare fraud is a bigger business in South Florida than the drug trade and safer. *60 Minutes* did an expose on this problem in 2011 and really made the government look inept. The number of phony Medicare "providers" was appalling and the thieves had no overhead. One of the individuals who was arrested admitted making $20 million (in a matter of months) and when being interviewed suggested there would be somebody to take his place. And yet the Obama administration claims the Bush era tax cuts are costing the Treasury $700 billion (over 10 years) is a problem. Anybody who passed 4th grade can "do the math" and see that equates to $70 billion a year, which was somehow a national disgrace, yet they can squander $60 Billion a year ($600 Billion over 10 years) and it doesn't even get an honorable mention by liberal talking heads. Sixty billion is just somebody's estimate. Sixty-Minutes did not provide a detailed calculation. Being the cynic I am I'd guess the problem is a lot worse, but represents 10% of the Medicare budget and only five days of what the government spends. Yet we can't cut, reform or modernize Medicare because our seniors would be without care. Hogwash and scare tactics. (Remember they are convinced you're stupid)

"The federal government's system for analyzing Medicare and Medicaid data for possible fraud are inadequate and underused, making it more difficult to detect the billions of dollars in fraudulent claims paid out each year...."[33]

The crawler at the end of the *60 Minutes* story suggested the person responsible for fraud detection "resigned". She should have been in jail for dereliction of duty and impersonating a government official. This is an obvious example of how, by stop wasting money politicians can stop taxing people.

---

[33]   Pensacola New Journal, AP, Kelli Kennedy, July 13, 2011

9) Have done nothing to reform immigration. Eleven million illegals in the country who broke the law, are breaking other laws, and will not be deported. What is the penalty for their having broken the law? I wonder how many phony voter registration cards the politicians gave these people? How unsafe are the country's borders? Now thousands of children are coming in. Texas and Arizona know the borders aren't secure and it's long past time to build/finish a wall.

10) On a daily basis spend $11 billion before 3 o'clock, 25-50% of which is documentable waste. What is the true cost of running the government? Aren't there more civilized ways to steal from the public than an income tax? And why isn't that money raised and USED closer to home? (city, county, state)

11) Continue to aid and abet the existence of a terrorist organization, namely the IRS, on a daily basis.

12) Have been running a giant Ponzi scheme since 1935 and chastised Governor Perry for calling it exactly that during his 2012 campaign. They've had 80 years to get it right and it's broke. They've blown every estimate, cost analysis, life expectancy and projection that was ever created. This is an issue the "Occupy" crowd should have taken on.

13) Have had 248 years (since 1775) to fix the US Postal Service and it's broke.

14) Have waged a War on Poverty since 1964. They had 50+ years to get it right. $1 trillion of taxpayer money is confiscated each year by the income tax, transferred to the poor and yet they want more.

15) Ignored abuses in Medicare and Medicaid (established in 1955). They've had 60 years to get it right and both are broke.

16) Established Freddie Mac in 1970 and they've had 45 years to get it right and it's broke.

17) Have watched the Department of Energy (created in 1977 to lessen our dependence on foreign oil) balloon to over 16,000 employee and a budget of $30 billion and until recently we still imported more oil every year. They had 37 years to get it right and it's a waste of money.

The federal government only has four sources of revenues: a) stealing it from the citizenry through taxes and user fees) b) selling assets (i.e. guns, military hardware and other weapons of mass destruction) c) borrowing it (i.e. printing it), and d) charging interest (that it struggles to collect). As a side note to the "selling assets" source, the government has plenty of land, buildings, airstrips, highways, abandoned property and national parks it could sell or lease to "enhance revenues". Unfortunately some of those properties are polluted. Former Governor Jesse Ventura did an interesting investigative piece about one such property known as Plum Island (NY) (Wikipedia). There appears to be a major cover-up surrounding it.

Nearly ten percent of the federal budget is now spent to pay the interest on the debt the Republi-crats have amassed. That's money that doesn't provide one product or service but is "penance" for the excess spending of past administrations. "We the people" get nothing in return. It does put money in the pockets of foreign bankers. The scarier scenario is what happens when interest rates rise to some more realistic amount. Even at 4% the interest on a $20 trillion debt would be $800 billion a year. That's double the combined budgets of the Departments of Commerce, Education, Homeland Security, HUD, Energy, Labor and (In)Justice, though too much of their budgets is wasted on overpaid, pay-check stealing bureaucrats, who have better benefits than the private sector. (A 2013 radio ad campaign in Southwest Florida for Border Patrol openings suggested that possible applicants should also consider "the federal benefits package" when making a career choice.)

Four of those departments could be abolished and nobody would miss them. Our kids would be smarter, housing cheaper, business more competitive, jobs more plentiful and America wouldn't be a police state. The Federal Reserve has had to manipulate interest rates down to the lowest in my lifetime just to keep the deficit (and the debt) from getting totally out of sight. Yet the economy isn't booming, wages are stagnant and small businesses are struggling. I'm fascinated by the idea of anybody lending the U.S. government/taxpayers money through a ten-year treasury note that pays a paltry 2% rate of interest. But even worse is the idea of the banks charging you to handle your money instead of pay you for being dumb enough to give it to them. Politicians think you're stupid especially with your lack of knowledge of basic economics.

And yet Americans want to vote for a "Republic-crat" and let them run the health care system. Go figure. Believe it or not, majorities are not always right. Before the great flood only one man had the sense to get out of the rain. Centuries later another man thought the world was round when the prevailing wisdom said otherwise.

Former President Nixon once said "What made America great has NOT been what government has done for the people but what the people have done for themselves". JFK's famous inaugural address quote "Ask not what your country can do for you, but what you can do for your country" wouldn't be a Democratic/Progressive mantra now.

When he wrote The Declaration of Independence Thomas Jefferson said, "When in the course of human events it becomes necessary…." NEWS FLASH: it's now necessary. He also said "A little rebellion now and then is a good thing, and as necessary in the political world as storms in the physical". It needs to be a ballot box rebellion, not a physical rebellion.

So who's to blame? Anyone who votes to keep an incumbent.

CHAPTER THREE

NO ACCOUNTABILITY

Before the election of 2010 I believed every sitting member of Congress with the exception of Congressman Dr. Ron Paul and Senator Dr. Tom Coburn earned one of the dirtbag, liar or power freak monikers. (Both have since retired) Prime examples were Joe Lieberman (2006), Lisa Murkowski (2010) and Arlen Specter (2010), and ex-Florida governor Charlie Christ (2010). The voters' sent them a message, "We want somebody else". Instead these four decided the voters were stupid and couldn't imagine how they would throw them out or dismiss them. So the Specter changed parties (and later died), Lieberman and Christ ran as independents and Murkowski as a write in. The voters of Alaska and Connecticut bought into it, Pennsylvania and Florida did not. "Chain-gang Charlie" switched parties and ran for unsuccessfully for governor of Florida in 2014 as a Democrat.

A few that deserve mention for having stayed to long or waited for a private sector "promotion" are: Harry Reid (D-NV), Charlie Rangel (D-NY), John Dingell (-MI), Thad Cochran (R-MS), Chris Dodd (D-CT) and Barney Frank (D-MA). Thankfully two of them retired, but it is beyond comprehension that there is no one in the Harlem area (NY-District 13) who is qualified to be a Congressperson except tax cheat, Charlie Rangel. Forty plus years? John Dingell, 59 years? I think this gives credibility to the notion the public has that politicians are all crooks, but he's OUR crook.

Harry Reid became the most powerful member of the US Senate because he lives in a small population state (Nevada) where 75% of the population lives within 50 miles of his home town and the Vegas unions keep him in power. He actually stood in front of a microphone championing the Cowboy Poetry Society as an essential government expenditure during the budget debate of 2011. Was nobody else in Nevada qualified to be a senator? Thankfully he's now retired.

If someone wanted to run against any of the dozens of dirtbags, liars, and power freaks they would have to deal with the character assassination/ negative campaign ads that will be heaped on them since none of their incumbent opponents can run on the record I just outlined (I give you Hilary Clinton and the 2016 presidential race). It's a shame the media tolerates and even fosters negative ads. Yankee Capitalism at its worst. The noble thing to do would be hold candidates to a higher standard and accept only on-point, solution oriented, issue related ads and responses to their questions.

Mandatory reading for every high school history, civics, American government type class in addition to the books I've mentions should be everything they can get their hands on about government waste. I've included an excerpt from the 656 page report of the Grace Commission requested by President Reagan in 1981. (The underlines and notations are my own) Sadly, the report is gathering dust somewhere in Washington, D.C. A great class project would be to write a snail-mail certified letter to both of the states' US Senators and local Congress-critter and ask what they are doing about it.

January 12, 1984

The Honorable Ronald Reagan
President of the United States
The White House
Washington, D.C.

Dear Mr. President,

Following your directive to identify and suggest remedies for waste and abuse in the Federal Government, the President's Private Sector Survey (PPSS) offers recommendations which would save:

$424 billion in three years, rising to

$1.9 trillion per year(by the year 2000)

These proposals would transform the Federal debt situation as follows:

	Federal Debt (\$ trillions)		Annual Interest on Federal Debt (\$ billions)	
	Without PPSS	With PPSS	Without PPSS	With PPSS
1990	\$ 3.2	\$2.0	\$ 252.3	\$89.2
1995	6.2	2.2	540.9	62.3
2000	13.0	2.5	1,520.7	75.1

You asked the American people to help you get the Government "off their backs." If the American people realized how rapidly Federal Government spending is likely to grow under existing legislated programs, I am convinced they would compel their elected representatives to "get the Government off their backs." In our survey to search out ways to cut costs in the Government, great emphasis was placed on the spending outlook, which is as follows:

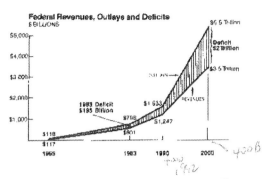

Federal Revenues, Outlays and Deficits
$ BILLIONS

If fundamental changes are not made in Federal spending, as compared with the fiscal 1983 deficit of $195 billion, a deficit of over ten times that amount, $2 trillion, is projected for the year 2000, only 17 years from now. In that year, the Federal debt would be $13.0 trillion ($160,000 per current taxpayer) and the interest alone on the debt would be $1.5 trillion per year ($18,500 per year per current taxpayer).

Mr. President, these projections are the result of a joint effort between PPSS and a leading U.S. economic forecasting firm. They are the result of very careful study and drove us to seek out every possible savings opportunity, a "like tireless bloodhounds," as you requested.

In the course of the search by our 36 Task Forces, chaired by 161 top executives from around the country and staffed by over 2,000 volunteers that they provided, we came up with 2,478 separate, distinct, and specific recommendations which are the basis for the carefully projected savings. For practical purposes, these savings, if fully implemented, could virtually eliminate the reported deficit by the 1990's versus an alternative deficit of $10.2 trillion in the decade of the 1990's if no action is taken.

Equally important, the 2,478 cost-cutting, revenue-enhancing recommendations we have made can be achieved without raising taxes, without weakening America's needed defense build-up, and without in any way harming necessary social welfare programs.

Because we are starting from a deficit of $195 billion, every dollar we can stop spending is a dollar that the Government does not have to borrow. With future Government borrowing costs at 11 percent (versus 10.75 percent now and 14.5 percent when you took office) and inflation taken at 6 percent per year over the longer run, these savings compound quickly.

Applying these interest and inflation rates, the result is that a dollar saved today accumulates to $32 over 12 years and $71 over 17 years. Thus, any potential saving made, as compared to not making the saving, translates into a difference in cumulative spending of 32 times that amount through 1995 and 71 times that amount through the end of the century.

Therefore, $100 billion in reduced Government spending in year one equates cumulatively to

$7.1 trillion in the year 2000. And since borrowings are decreased by this amount, so will the national debt decrease.

This is, of course, a horrendous prospect. If the American people understood the gravity of the outlook, they would not, I believe, support representatives who might let it happen.

Mr. President, you have been so correct in resisting attempts to balance the budget by increasing taxes. The tax load on the average American family is already at counterproductive levels with the underground economy having now grown to an estimated $500 billion per year, costing about $100 billion in lost Federal tax revenues per year.

The size of the underground economy is understandable when one considers that median family income taxes have increased from $9 in 1948 to $2,218 in 1983, or by 246 times. This is runaway taxation at its worst.

Importantly, any meaningful increases in taxes from personal income would have to come from lower and middle income families, as 90 percent of all personal taxable income is generated below the taxable income level of $35,000.

Further, there isn't much more that can be extracted from high income brackets. If the Government took 100 percent of all taxable income beyond the $75,000 tax bracket not already taxed, it would get only $17 billion, and this confiscation, which would destroy productive enterprise, would only be sufficient to run the Government for seven days.

Resistance to additional income taxes would be even more widespread if people were aware that:

One-third of all their taxes is consumed by waste and inefficiency in the Federal Government as we identified in our survey. Another one-third of all their taxes escapes collection from others as the underground economy blossoms in direct proportion to tax increases and places even more pressure on law abiding taxpayers, promoting still more underground economy—a vicious cycle that must be broken.

With two-thirds of everyone's personal income taxes wasted or not collected, 100 percent of what is collected is absorbed solely by interest on the Federal debt and by Federal Government contributions to transfer payments. In other words, all individual income tax revenues are gone before one nickel is spent on the services which taxpayers expect from their Government.

Our survey studied the small as well as the major items of cost savings, items of broad national impact as well as those of a more localized nature. I believe you will be interested in a few random examples of what we found:

In the Northwest, the Federal Power Marketing Administration is selling subsidized power at one-third of market rates. If the Federal power were priced at market, there would be a three-year increase in revenues of $4.5 billion, which equates to the three-year personal income

PPSS Savings Recommendations

	$ Billions	% of Total
Program Waste	$160.9	37.9%
System Failures	151.3	35.7
Personnel Mismanagement	90.9	21.4
Structural Deficiencies	12.7	3.0
Other Opportunities	8.6	2.0
Total	$424.4	100.0%

These data confirm our findings that system failures and personnel mismanagement together comprise well over one-half 57.1 percent, of the total savings possibilities. They are at the foundation of inefficiencies in the Federal Government. Program waste, which accounts for 37.9 percent of the savings recommendations, would also be substantially eliminated if proper systems and personnel management were in place.

The above underscores one of our most important recommendations, which is the establishment of an Office of Federal Management in the Executive Office of the President. This Federal Government top management office would include OMB, GSA and OPM and have Government-wide responsibility for establishing, modernizing, and monitoring management systems.

If it is set up and staffed properly, it could go a long way to avoid in the future the thousands of deficiencies and examples of waste that we have identified. We would not feel our task complete if we just identified past deficiencies without recommendations for a management and organizational structure that would be best suited for preventing the errors of the past.

Additionally, the establishment of this new office would be beneficial in the implementation process of the PPSS recommendations.

In this regard, we believe that your Cabinet Council on Management and Administration, working in concert with the Office of Cabinet Affairs, is uniquely suited to lead a Government-wide effort to restore sound principles of management and efficiency to the Federal Government. While the Cabinet Council already has taken a leadership role in this regard, we urge you to call upon it to make implementation of the PPSS recommendations Government-wide its highest priority.

Mr. President, it was a great honor to have been asked by you to engage in this effort to identify ways to eliminate inefficiency, waste and abuse in the Federal Government. The project was structured and staffed to effect enduring improvement so that our children and grandchildren would not inherit a situation that would be devastating to them and to the values of our economic and social system. It was in this vein that we were able to enlist the 161 top executives from private business and other organizations to chair and to staff our 36 Task Forces at a cost to the private sector of over $75 million and at no cost to the Government.

All the participants join with me in thanking you for the opportunity to be of service and in looking forward to whatever additional help we may be able to provide to assure that the greatest practical results are obtained from the work of this Commission.

Respectfully,

J. Peter Grace
Chairman

Take special note of the comment "...every dollar we can stop spending is a dollar they don't have to borrow". That was 30+ years ago, and it's even truer today.

As a point of reference, if person has a job that pays on average $50,000 a year (about $24.50/hr. for a 40 hour week) they would have to work 20 years just to have earned $1 million dollars (before taxes). If a person were able to work for the 40 or 50 years from the time they graduated high school/college your total earnings would be about $2.5 million. Someone whose income averaged $100,000 a year most of their working life would earn $4-$5 million. That may sounds like a lot as a flat number but a person has to go to work, get aggravated, put up with organizational idiocy, arrange daycare, fight the traffic, pay for parking and kiss butt to make that money.

Forget the whole idea of a billion dollars. Someone would have to live forever, or start an internet company, to earn that much. If you think about one billion of something as time, here's a fact:

One billion seconds ago, Ronald Reagan was our president.

One billion minutes ago Jesus had only been gone from this planet about 70 years. (100 AD)

One billion hours ago dinosaurs were still 75,000 years from making an appearance.

Sadly the dirtbags, liars & power freaks spending taxpayer money don't even get concerned until they're talking about a hundred billion dollars which is about 3% of the budget. Anything less is chump change, tip money, a rounding error or trivial in the scheme of government waste. My point is that Congress spends $7,000,000 per minute which is more than tens of millions of people earn in a lifetime, yet Americans let them waste at least 25% of it. When are voters going to get concerned? While America may be the greatest country on Earth it should be even better.

The Obama administration is doing an outstanding job of doubling the debt in eight years, but had the audacity to call his predecessor (Bush 43) unpatriotic for adding about four trillion to it over his eight years.

The national debt has been rising steadily since 1980:

Dec. 31, 1980 Debt $1 Trillion Democrats control Congress

1981 to Dec. 31, 1992 (12 years Reagan/Bush) $4.2 Trillion Democrats control Congress

1993 to Dec. 31, 2000 (Clinton) $5.8 Trillion Republicans control Congress

2001 to Dec. 31, 2008 (Bush 43) $9.9 Trillion Both had Control/new war on Terror

Dec. 31, 2016 (Obama after 7 years) $19+ Trillion Democrats Control for 2 years/ Divided for 4 years/Reps 2 yrs.

You can draw your own conclusions about who the most wasteful president or Congress was/is but this issue cannot be ignored much longer. The 47% that weren't going to vote for Romney, but will vote for Hilary are not going to do anything about this.

Right now the country is allegedly recovering from the worse economic recession since the great depression and there is nothing on the horizon that says having thrown away billions that anything has turned around, contrary to what Washington is hyping. Most of the population would agree that one million dollars is still a lot of money, and we're in debt a million times a million, 19 times over. That equates to about $55,000+ for every man, woman and child in America the day you are born into this society. (Please make your check payable to the U.S. Treasury) One of my fellow vacationers at Camp Swampy who claimed to be neither a Democrat or a Republican but a capitalist, became a grandpa while we were there and he was outraged that the child came into this world $47,000 in debt.

Sadly elected officials simply ignore waste, nobody goes to jail, damn few get fired, nobody loses their pension, and even fewer are forced to resign. The media doesn't find it newsworthy enough to get involved with a daily story about waste and then follow it until it's resolved. The budget can be balanced thru cutting waste, but that translates into a lot of overpaid, paycheck stealing, unionized bureaucrats being unemployed (which liberals claim will damage the economy). That's a real shame, but nowhere near the shame of private sector workers losing their jobs, homes, health benefits and families because Washington has to take care of itself first. According to the Office of Personnel Management, in 2012, here are over 4.3 million people on the government payroll[34] (1.5 million military and the rest civilian) plus consultants and private contractors. At an average cost to the taxpayers of $100,000 each that's $430B. When those collecting a pension are factored in the number almost doubles. One fifth of the budget is for bodies, many of which are/were incompetent, useless, unionized, overpaid, favors to campaign contributors and power freaks.

I want to puke every time I hear liberal claims that the only way we can balance the budget is for the rich to pay more and that the only reason we have deficits is that the rich aren't paying their fair share. We have deficits because Congress doesn't have the balls to pass a balance budget amendment, give the president line item veto power, make hard choices and tell the public the truth, "we're broke, and we can't afford it". But we're still trying to buy your vote. For the record the Democrats controlled both houses of Congress and the White House in 2009 and 2010. If they didn't like the tax laws or tax rates why didn't they pass a bill to change them?

During the debate in early 2013 about the sequester many of the talking heads" on the liberal/Democratic side actually believed that cutting $85

---

[34]   www.opm.gov/policy-data

Billion from a budget of over $3.7 Trillion would have a catastrophic effect on the economy. Why is it "trickle-down economics" was chastised when President Reagan suggested cutting taxes, but just fine when President Obama engaged in fear-mongering about the sequester of 2013? Medi-scare has $60 billion of waste/fraud each year. That's only one program. With at least 25% ($900+ BILLION) being wasted, what is $85 Billion? 2.4% of the whole budget? Every entity can find that much waste, especially governments.

Some examples of waste making news in the past few year from Citizens against Government Waste (CAGW):

1) 82 federal programs to improve teacher quality (which the federal government has no business in)
2) 80 programs to help disadvantaged people with transportation
3) 80 programs for economic development
4) 47 programs for job training and employment
5) 20 separate programs to help the homeless, and
6) 15 different agencies overseeing food-safety laws

Going to the Citizens against Government Waste website should really make one sick and question why they pay even one dollar in taxes. Then ask why Congress couldn't have wasted some of that money on you. Ask why you lost your job, your house, your health insurance, were turned down for a loan and it takes $2-$5 to buy a gallon of gas. What average citizens need is "chump-change" compared to what is wasted every day in Washington.

In 2012 former Senator Coburn issued a report that says billions in federal funds will be spent to by the Department of Education to administer 230 programs. They include Early Reading First, Striving Readers, Reading First, Reading is Fundamental, Even Start, Head Start, Early Head Start, Homeless Education, Native Hawaiian Education, Alaska Native Education, Rural Education, Indian Education, Historic Whaling Education, and Trading Partners etc... And Kids still can't read. Just more fodder to justify abolishing this department and putting the education back at the lowest possible level of oversight. Not necessarily the government.

How many of those anti-poverty programs have lifted the poor out of their addiction to the government handouts? Why trust the government with more of your money when they've done such a poor job managing what you had stolen in the past? Since when are higher taxes an incentive for anyone to take a risk or invest in America?

Other headline grabbing examples of waste, fraud and corruption are:

a) Soleyndra, b) FHA mortgages c) IRS phony refunds, d) overpaid unemployment claims, e) a breach of a $100M security system at a New York airport, f) Pensions and raises for staff, g) the whole concept of base line budgeting h) taxpayer money and gangs involved in tax fraud, i) campaigns to lie about each other, call each other names and invent issues that ignore the real problems this country faces.

I would like to know why the taxpayers are sponsoring a cycling team or race cars when people are without medical care, food, housing and birth control pills!

Senator Rand Paul (2012) brought up the age old problem that NOBODY READS THIS STUFF. He was holding up a 600 page bill that no one had read and yet the Senate was going to vote on the bill that day. Their own rules call for the bill to be posted on the internet for 48 hours before a final vote. It may not be possible to read, much less digest, the legalese in a 600 page bill in 48 hours. However, this bill was typical of the "Christmas tree" bills that come out of Congress. They contain provisions that have nothing to do with the theme of the original legislation. The most famous quote on that subject was that of the former Speaker of the House, Princess Nancy, when referring to the 2000 plus page bill affectionately known as Obama-care, "We have to pass this bill so that we can find out what's in it." What's in it? What an asinine comment. It's her job to know what's in it before she shoves it down her constituents' throats and twists arms to get it passed.

Every day there is a new story about waste, fraud or corruption. A book like this is a never ending story, yet "We the People" refuse to hold elected officials accountable in the one way they don't expect, THROW THE BUMS OUT.

....

CHAPTER FOUR

THE D'S WERE IN CONTROL

After fourteen years of controlling Congress the Republicans snatched defeat from the jaws of victory in November, 2006. On January 3, 2007 the Democrats took back control of the Congress. They had control of the budget process for 2008 and 2009. They controlled the Senate and White House (2/3 of the process) from January, 2009 to December, 2014. In the first year they had to deal with George Bush who forced them to compromise on spending and spending increases. Many of them were insignificant. In 2008 House Speaker Nancy Pelosi and Senate Leader Harry Reid simply passed continuing resolutions to keep the government running until Obama could take over the presidency. Then Congress passed "catch-all" spending bills to run the government until October 2009. The Democrats have not passed a <u>balanced</u> budget since. The R's didn't pass on for '15 and '16 when they had control of Congress after the '14 elections. Proposing massive deficits isn't something they should be proud of or can run on.

In 2010 came all the hype about a government shutdown. In 2012 and 2013 it happened again. Following the logic that they think you're stupid, they make outlandish claims to scare the public about the government not issuing social security checks, paying Medicare claims, or issuing tax refunds. Isn't it amazing the government is going to withhold the people's money from them, their "guaranteed" benefits (as Obama claimed about Medicare during the 2012 campaign) and a lawful tax refund, rather than withhold the pay of Congress, White House staff, federal judges, or IRS agents. The dirtbags aren't going to shut down the military, Homeland Security, IRS, FBI, DEA, CIA, prisons, air traffic control, or Congressional staff, yet they threaten to disrupt the vacations and travel plans of people who visit museums, national parks and tourist attractions.

I'm sure the government fears the fact that if they did shut down any government agency or furlough one of those "non-essential" paycheck stealing bureaucrats the citizenry would find out we can get along just fine without it/them and solidify the fact that they are overpaid, paycheck stealers.

A 2011 USA Today article authored by Dennis Cauchon entitled "Federal Benefits, Pensions Explode" said "The government paid $268 billion in pension and health benefits in 2010 to 10 million former civil "servants", military personnel and their dependents, about $100 billion MORE than a decade ago after adjusting for inflation. And $7 billion more was deposited into tax-deferred accounts of current workers". But here's the best part, "the government added to the FUTURE costs:

a) $107 Billion in retirement benefits accumulated by current workers,
b) $106 Billion in new benefits granted to veterans,
c) More than $300 billion in the snowballing expense of previous retirement promises that have no source of funding.

In all, the government committed more money to the 10 million former public "servants" (yeah right) in 2010 than the $690 billion it paid to 54 million Social Security beneficiaries."

Pensions and health care are about third of the Defense department's budget. How would the country be less safe if we cut what went to people who wasted the money? Robert Gates, a former Secretary of Defense said the costs "are eating us alive".

For every elected official drawing a paycheck there is at least one former official drawing a pension check (except former Congressmen Ron Paul and Howard Coble). We have 5 ex-presidents, 6 ex-Vice-presidents if you count Bush 41, and thousands of Senators, Congressmen/women, cabinet secretaries and high ranking military members. The five ex-presidents alone cost taxpayers over $12 million a year. How many do we need to support? For how long? Why can't they get a real job?? The there's "slick-Willie" who's making millions giving speeches. So why does he need anything from the taxpayers?

The minimum wage should have been raised many years ago and probably indexed for inflation. When I was first entering the working world minimum wage was $2.50 per hour, gas was. 33 cents a gallon not $3.30. A loaf of bread about. 50 cents not $3. A new car (Ford Maverick) was $2,000, not $15,000. My first house cost $25,000 now the median price in the country is closer to $200,000. Has the minimum wage gone up? 10 times? 6 times? any times??? In terms of purchasing power (Thank you Federal Reserve) it has actually gone down. I wonder if there are any believable independent studies on how many people in this country actually get paid less than $10 an hour.

I affectionately call "minimum wage", "show up wages" because if the person you hired shows up consider yourself lucky. I wouldn't bet on getting much work out of them though. That mentality was prevalent at Club Fed among inmates who felt that for 12 cents an hour, showing up was about all they were going to do. Some expended more energy trying to get out of work than actually working. People earning minimum wage will always have their eye open for another job and whatever time an employer spent training them will be for naught.

CHAPTER FIVE

MEDIA HEADLINES

During my vacation at Club Fed I began to collect research for this book from publications that came to the camp. (The Wall Street Journal, USA Today, local newspapers and various business oriented magazines) Many inmates would subscribe to them and then pass them around when they were done. My family also sent me dozens of articles from the local newspapers.

I made a list of some quotes from the dozens or articles I collected which support what I believed. Here are just a few of the highlights about the dirtbags, liars and power freaks that are (were) running the government:

a) Custom officials "we do not have enough resources to handle all these problems. Our agency is confronted with more violations than we can address" after the ICE director issued a memo to use "prosecutorial discretion" for illegals who have been students after Obama used an executive order to enact the controversial "dream act". In short they broke our law but don't prosecute them, don't fine them and deport them. That sounds like "selective enforcement" to me. (And I went to prison for a victimless alleged crime).

b) After 200 years the House of Representative abolished the "page" program. It was a waste of $5 Million in the electronic age. Let's see the budget is $3.7 Trillion, $5 million is about 1 seconds of what it cost to run the government. But this was 100% waste.

c) H & R Block could no longer make "rapid refund" loans (2011) because their lender (HSBC) was ordered by regulators to stop ripping off the public with high interest loans. What took you so long? (H & R Block actually charged more than I did for doing tax returns yet knew nothing about tax planning or small business)

d) 70% of Medicaid dollars go the elderly and disabled, not the poor and single mothers. Every day we find a way to extend life we did a bigger hole for Social Security, Medi-scare and Medicaid. When these programs were established life expectancy was hardly 65, now it's either in the mid 70's or 80's depending on whether you believe the medical profession or the IRS.

e) The tax code is so complex that the former chairman of the tax-writing committee (C. Rangel-D, NY), like millions of Americans, cannot be confident he can properly perform, unassisted, the duty of paying taxes. Since when is it a duty? Keeping accurate records has nothing to do with preparation.

f) When they find savings they only talk in terms of one year. If I were one of those demonized rich people I'd want to know why I'm paying taxes that go to support a criminal activity and why the person in charge of fraud detection isn't out of a job and in jail for the gross mismanagement of public money and dereliction of duty.

g) Seventy-two (72,000) thousand stimulus payments went to DEAD people. (Stephen Ohlemacher, AP, Oct. 8, 2008). "More than 89,000 stimulus payments of $250 each went to people who were either dead or in prison......." Here's the best part. THERE IS NO PROVISION IN THE LAW TO RECOVER PAYMENTS INCORRECTLY SENT TO DEAD PEOPLE. "Based on the failure of the Social Security Administration to PROPERLY check its records AND CONGRESS' failure to fully think through the provisions needed to govern these payments, SSA lost $22.3 million in American tax dollars"...

Sen. Tom Coburn R- Ok. I know it's only $250 per person but what else could we have done with $22 million? How about health care for children?

h) Obama's vacations. Money to China for abortions.

OTHER HEADLINES:

Oct. 14, 2010, former Congressman Jim Traficant in a piece titled "John Q", "The Internal Revenue Service must also be abolished. And our Government must REPLACE our tax-revenue scheme, NOT "reform it". That must be done with a consumption tax.

Feb. 2011-Warren (Ohio) Tribune editorial - Be worried about the future. If you were born after 1957 and expect to live to be 80 or beyond, Social Security as it operates presently will NOT be there for you. "What's in the trust fund"[35]. "..Congress has been tapping this (Social Security money) revenue stream for years, while handing out IOU's—"special issue" Treasury Bonds—to the Social Security Trust Fund. ….these special-issue bonds can only be redeemed by raising taxes, cutting spending elsewhere or borrowing-which the government would have to do if the Trust Fund didn't exist. This year (2010), for the first time since the 1980s the payroll tax didn't produce enough money to pay current benefits, forcing officials to tap general revenues".

Feb. 2011-Warren Tribune- IRS isn't stopping tax credits. Erroneous EIC payments.

Jan. 2011-Marietta (Oh) Times. Cracking Down on Fraud. Throughout the nation, enterprising convicts have conned the IRS out of a whopping $123M during the past 5 years. The IRS itself ADMITS that in 2009, 45,000 fraudulent tax returns were filed by prison inmates. (Ya gotta luv it).

---

[35] Kansas City Star, Dec. 17, 2010 appearing the Youngstown, (Oh) Vindicator

Feb. 2011-Associated Press. Appeared in the Youngstown (Oh) Vindicator. Dozens Charged with Medicare fraud. (A few of the guys I knew at Camp Swampy were there for Medicare Fraud). $60B a year business according to a 60 minutes story and safer than trafficking drugs according to the masterminds.

March 2011- Associated Press (YV) - GOP Hopefuls, Cut it or shut it.

Feb. 2011-Newsday writer A. Bessent (YV). Overhaul federal tax code. Doesn't everybody want a simpler tax code? My fantasy is scrapping the whole thing and replacing it with a consumption tax—national sales tax, maybe or a value added tax (GOD forbid). Getting from here to there would be a daunting, and you'd have to be fair for low-income workers (Obviously he hasn't read the Fair Tax). But imagine a world with no taxes withheld from your paycheck, no tax forms to file and NOOOOOO IRS.

Dec.2010 - Cal Thomas, columnist-Make Congress part-time. Returning home shouldn't mean flying home for long weekends and then coming back to Washington. IT should mean returning to a real job where the member can't raise his own pay, receive top medical care a reduced or no cost, print and spend other people's money, or count on others to pay into his retirement fund. If he owned a business, he would have to meet a payroll and balance the budget. The member would also have to rely on Social Security, like other Americans.

March 2011. Youngstown (Oh)Vindictor article. Bill would tie lawmakers' pay to unemployment rate. (Sounds good to me).

March 2011. Gregory Rodriguez, LA Times. Behold hidden welfare state. The writer presents the opinion of a Cornell political scientist that suggested IRAs, the mortgage interest deduction and employer paid health insurance are a hidden welfare state. While those who avail themselves of these LEGITIMATE opportunities it's the same as getting a check from the government. Let's get to the national sales tax.

CHAPTER SIX

THE GIANT PONZI SCHEME

Social Security system is at the top of my list of the lies the government tells the country. Anybody between 22 and 40 should be demanding their money back and that paying into this giant Ponzi scheme be voluntary. It's dumbfounding to me that a person would vote for a presidential candidate because they could get free birth control pills and yet have 6% of their paycheck confiscated under the guise that if they live long enough the money will come back to them. The money definitely won't buy what a dollar they lose buys and if they don't make it to retirement age the money goes back into the "trust fund" probably to pay for somebody who didn't contribute. Originally Social Security was a voluntary system and the original social security cards said very clearly, NOT FOR IDENTIFICATION. (This is not some internet manipulation or creation)

History Lesson on Your Social Security Card

Just in case some of you young whippersnappers (and some older ones) didn't know this. It's easy to check out, if you don't believe it. Be sure and show it to your family and friends. They need a little history lesson on what's what and it doesn't matter whether you are <u>Democrat or Republican.</u> <u>Facts are Facts.</u>

<u>Social Security Cards up until the 1980s expressly stated the number and</u> <u>Card were not to be used for identification purposes.</u> Since nearly everyone in the

United States now has a number, it became convenient to use it anyway *and the*

message. NOT FOR IDENTIFICATION, was removed.

<u>An old Social Security card with the "NOT FOR IDENTIFICATION"</u> <u>message.</u>

Our Social Security

Today the letters "SSN" probably stand for "slave surveillance number" because once a person or their parents' apply for that number the government owns you. So what happened? The government lied and people were on their way to becoming financial slaves.

Social Security's latest lie is that it has plenty of assets (a special class of Treasury Bonds) to cover its needs. The liars won't tell you the only way for them to "cash in" those bonds is for the government to redeem them, using income tax revenues.[36]

In my rookie year as an accountant the maximum earnings subject to the social security "tax" was $7,800 and the percent they were stealing from each employee was 4.2%. The employer matched the employee "contribution" amount as they still do today. For those that were self-employed the "tax" was 7.9%. If this isn't a giant Ponzi scheme why is the maximum for earnings now $113,700 and the rate 12.4%? Could it be politicians never "invested" the money? Never "locked it away" from dirtbags, liars and power freaks? Missed every estimate ever contrived? Pay billions in questionable disability claims? Pay children of a deceased parent until age 26? Never expected people to live past 65 much less 85?

I hope people realize that everyday science and medicine finds a way to extend life even one month it further bankrupts the system. Yet women's reproductive rights get more media coverage. When you get past 50 how many women need abortions or birth control pills anyway? Are you brain dead?? I was appalled that Congress even entertained the women who made this case when we have so many other <u>American</u> issues that need addressed.

A really baffling aspect of Social Security's financial crisis is that Congress passed a "tax holiday" in 2009 and actually took less money from people's earnings. That was money that was supposed to go to Social Security. It's broke, is underfunded and the politicians put less money in the system. Taxpayers were given their own money as though it was "manna from

---

[36]   Kansas City Star, *What's in the Trust Fund*, Dec. 17, 2010

Obama" yet it simply abetted the bankrupting of the system and your retirement.

Social Security was originally sold to the public as being tax free when one was eligible to collect it. In 1992 when "Slick Willie" needed to "enhance revenues" he proposed "means testing" social security recipients. If someone didn't really need it, they wouldn't get it. It was a concept proposed by Ross Perot in his 1992 presidential campaign. With the full blessing of the AARP (that giant insurance company that allegedly looks out for seniors) Congress passed a bill that would tax a portion of a person's social security "benefits" if their income as a couple exceeded $32,000, or $25,000 if single. At the time gas wasn't $3-$5 a gallon, bread wasn't $3 a loaf, and a mid-size car wasn't $30,000. Today $32,000 is poverty but the tax system suggests you're well off. The government practices "base line budgeting" to spend more money every year on wasteful programs and give raises to paycheck stealing bureaucrats. However they anguish about giving social security recipients a MEAGER cost of living adjustment (3 tenths of a percent in 2017). I have never belonged to AARP because they screwed every senior by sitting in their hands rather than opposing this law.

Here are FACTS about Social Security that most liberals/Democrats/ progressives choose to ignore:

Lie #1) when President Franklin Roosevelt introduced the program he PROMISED it would be completely voluntary.

Lie #2) Participants would only pay 1% of the first $1,400 of income. (Now it's 7.65% and $115K)

Lie #3) the money that people elected to put into the program would be TAX DEDUCTIBLE. (Changed by a Democratic Congress) (FYI, 401Ks and IRAs are tax deductible/tax deferred)

Lie #4) the money the participants put in would be put in the "INDEPENDENT TRUST FUND" and not the General Fund and would ONLY be used for Social Security

Retirement. Under President Johnson's (D) "Great Society" that stopped.

Lie #5) the payment would NEVER be taxed. Thank Clinton/Gore (D) for killing that.

Lie #6) now the program is being called a "government benefit". (The government ran out of the people's money and has to pay them out of the general fund)

All of the Democrats out there that want America to think it's the Republicans who want to tinker with Social Security benefits better look in the mirror. That voluntary part should be re-instated yesterday, but once any lie is told, another has to be told to cover up the first one.

In the 1970's immigrants from Europe and the Middle East came here and worked menial jobs or for family members so that they could collect just enough credits to get on the Social Security and Medicare rolls. At that time a person only needed 20 quarters of earnings (it's now 40) to be eligible for benefits. These people knew what they paid in was a pittance compared to what they would get back.

If a person invested the money confiscated from their earnings over the 40-45 years of their working life they would have a) a nest egg that they had control over and access to, b) a much larger monthly income, c) something to pass on to their heirs and d) flexibility to invest it as they wish. Try it yourself, assume someone earned an average of $50,000/yr. over their life time (assume 45 years). Let's also assume they can average 5% a year in appreciation, dividends or interest on the $3,100 (6.2% of $50k) they didn't give to the Ponzi scheme. That would accumulate to over $500,000. If only 3% a year was withdrawn it would last 33 years (without any further earnings) and the monthly check would be more than what SSA pays. It should arouse disgust for those people. The employer could give the employee the $3100 they don't have to match as either a pay raise or an IRA/401K account contribution.

Before the government tries to tell people that they also get disability coverage with their donation, my answer is buy your own, it's still cheaper. The process to get on social security disability is de-humanizing, filled with questionable claimants, and time consuming, yet there is an army of lawyers willing to take your case.

The government is always engaged in a propaganda campaign to show future retirees how to increase their social security benefits. There are only three solutions to the shortage that Social Security faces: a) the old-stand-by, increase taxes, b) reduce/delay payouts and c) thin out the herd. I don't think the tax side is going to get much traction, which forces the Social Security Administration to encourage delaying the collecting of benefits workers paid for and are entitled to.

Everyone is eligible to start collecting their benefits four years before their full retirement age (66/67). I tell everybody take the money as soon as they can. Why? If a retiree doesn't live those four extra years the money is gone. The only person who can get it is a surviving spouse assuming they had one, otherwise the money goes back into the social security "trust fund". If a retiree thinks they don't need the money, take it anyway and be disciplined enough to invest it so that by the time you reach their full retirement you can collect from the government and from the investment account. The combined checks could be the same benefit a person waited four years longer to collect. A retiree's monthly income could be adjusted by calling the investment fund manager not waiting for the Social Security Administration to deem seniors worthy of even a meager cost of living adjustment.

When the average monthly "benefit" check is about $1,100, over those four years the investment account could amass $40,000-$50,000 without one penny of earnings. Whether a retiree begins collecting at the earlier age or later age the social security death benefit, $255, is still the same. It hasn't been increased in the last 30 years.

The naysayers will suggest you could lose the money (probably due to inept government monetary policies) or that it might be subject to income tax (thank you AARP and Bill Clinton). Some planning and sound investing will minimize if not negate both of those.

THE DEBT

"Governments never have enough of our money and they'll never ask if we have enough. Whatever they do is sold as noble, even righteous and if people rebel they are uncaring and greedy".[37]

As Mr. Reese pointed out the country is in debt because the politicians want Americans in debt. We are therefore financial slaves and inflation their best friend. The government can pay off "good dollars" with cheap dollars as long as they have more money coming in each year, even if it's worth less.

The fiscal cliff is pure theater. The United States is the only country on the planet with a debt limit, which has never been adhered to and Congress is never going to pay down/off the debt. In street lingo they're just going to keep "paying the juice". I wonder what would happen if American taxpayers decided to pay ONLY the interest on their government backed mortgage, student loans, car loans or credit cards. They'd be the defendant in a lawsuit, homeless and probably walking that's what.

Politicians need to take a machete to the federal budget not just a pair of scissors. Realistically any meaningful cuts in federal spending ultimately means fewer paycheck stealing bureaucrats, smaller pensions, fewer moochers and fewer overpriced weapons of mass destruction. There is

---

[37]   Syndicated Columnist Cal Thomas, April 15, 2009, Youngstown Vindicator

enough waste to the balance the federal budget without raising anybody's taxes. However, they would have to violate the "11th "commandment, <u>Thou Shalt Not Displace a Fellow Bureaucrat</u>. It's OK if GM (when it was private) lays people off, or Hostess shuts down, or Microsoft sends jobs overseas, casinos shut down, cities teeter on bankruptcy, but don't you dare eliminate a federal government job.

The Biggest Boondoggle, How the Obama Administration could save $100 billion, [38] is an article by John Aquilla on the Navy's Gerald Ford class aircraft carrier. His point was "…the Defense Department's fixation on preserving legacy systems designed for a kind of war that the U.S. is likely never to fight again. The ship is $2 billion over budget and nobody gets fired or jailed.[39]

In an Article titled "Debt will hit young Americans" (Dec. 17, 2010) writers William Beach and Dustin Siggins of the Heritage Foundation make the point again that it's our children and grandchildren who will have to "carry the burden" of the impending fiscal free fall. (That's been the mantra since I qualified as one of those children and grandchildren) For those in their 20's that could be an extra $3,000 per year in taxes. The authors echo the point made by Margaret Thatcher, former Prime Minister of Great Britian, "when government runs out of other people's money, it can be a very bad thing". The authors suggest the national debt could really be $130 trillion. They are correct.

The article goes on that former Senator Tom Coburn (a medical doctor) has said there is a $100 billion per year of waste in Medicare and Medicaid. Congressman Ryan and former CBO director Alice Rivlin say they found $30 billion a year in Medicare alone. *60 Minutes* found $60 billion. Ron Paul and Barney Frank suggested there is $100 billion a year to be saved from wasteful defense spending. Congresswoman Jan Schakowsky suggested there was $90 billion a year. The Office of Management and Budget says there were $125 billion in IMPROPER

[38] John Aquilla, Dec. 8, 2008, Forbes
[39] Associated Press, Nov, 2013, Brock Vergakis

payments in 2009. The list goes on and on and on. When I hear all the dirtbags, liars & power freaks claim they can't cut defense, Medicare, Medicaid or government pensions I want to puke.

In a September, 2011 article[40] entitled *"Paying money to the dead"* by columnist and commentator Cal Thomas, "The problem is that once a federal agency or program is started, it is <u>easier</u> (my emphasis) to find an honest politician that it is to cut something from the budget". Mr. Thomas also suggested the Office of Personnel Management had paid out $600 million to dead federal retirees over five years. On an annual basis it was between $100 million and $150 million. In an age of instant information and instant communication and a whole network of financial spying how could those charged with oversight not know someone was deceased? Do the talking heads present this waste to voters on the nightly news, or the front page of the newspaper or some financial publication? Heavens no, we can't embarrass the government! "Essential vs. non-essential" federal employees labels, during the 2013 shutdown, begs the question "Why in the world are taxpayers paying these people"?

Doesn't the fact that you are paying 25% TOO MUCH in whatever taxes bother you? Or that those in control of the money should be a lot closer to home?? So voters can keep an eye on them? With over 2.5 million people on the federal payroll and probably at least that many collecting a pension maybe it's time to downsize. If these people are so valuable let the cities, counties or state government hire them. Sadly all of them are having financial problems also due to out of control health care costs, pensions and benefits and many are headed for bankruptcy (I give you Detroit). They <u>have to balance </u>their budgets and don't have a printing press to do it. A fellow inmate who used to be a high ranking official in the state government in Florida suggested they didn't want to hire former federal workers because they didn't want to work. Really?

Unfortunately, the people elected to city, state and county offices are no choir boys either. The residents of Bell, California were victimized by the

---

[40] Warren Tribune 9/27/11

outrageous salaries of their elected officials. Two of Illinois' most recent governors went to jail. Likewise a former Louisiana governor. Detroit filed for bankruptcy protection as did Jefferson, Alabama, Orange County, California, Harrisburg, Pa., Central Falls, RI and Boise County, ID. More are looming. Waste, fraud and abuse are an integral part of the problem.

An unverified item floating around the internet recently captioned "Why is the USA Bankrupt?" suggests illegal immigrants are costing taxpayers at all levels, city, states, county and federal over $300 billion dollars a year in welfare, food assistance, Medicaid, education, prosecution, incarceration and suppressed wages. We are not going to send them back, cannot incarcerate all of them and are passing up a chance to generate revenue by preaching against it. Let's charge every adult (over 18) a $5,000 fee to be given the opportunity to stay in this country and a $2,000 fee for each child, with the stipulation they become legally employed within 12 months. Then deportation becomes mandatory. How many billions do you think will that raise? Save?

The number of foreign countries that vote against us at the UN in endless yet we keep giving them "foreign aid". The blankets we had at Club Fed said "made in Pakistan". Cereal was from China. In 1968 George Wallace made a statement that this country spent more and more money on foreign aid and yet we had less and less friends around the world. While he certainly was racist, that statement was dead on, and still true today.

The Washington Times in Dec. 2012 reported. "Over the past decade, the public has been forced to shell out $57 Billion for an agency (TSA) that has made flying an ordeal. All the groping and indignities passengers have been subjected too has been for naught. TSA has never caught a single terrorist, yet it continues to insist on overspending BILLIONS (my emphasis) on pornographic screening machines. The European Union, by contrast, refuses to adopt the technology."

Congress was debating 60 bills to name post offices for an organization that has become a white elephant and is collapsing because of its pension and retirement commitments much the same as several states and the social security system. They had zero bills up for debate about who to fix the mess. Any long term solution involves a reduction in force, service and benefits. Sadly, again politicians assume they can continue to print their way out of it and make Americans bigger financial slaves.

The US Health care system wastes $750 billion a year most of which comes from Medicare, Medicaid and VA programs. That would sure cover a large chunk of the yearly federal deficit. The government recently attacked 91 people accused of committing Medicare fraud to the tune of $429 million. [41]Remember the governments spends $10 billion a day, a 25%--50% of which is waste. $429 million amounts to less than 5% of what's spent and less than 10% of the waste. The $429M was over a longer period of time which makes it even less relevant. A company the government "loaned" $249M to that made batteries (A123) went bankrupt recently[42]. Is anyone going to jail? One loan of $249 million versus 91 people involving $429 million, you do the math.

"A top executive from the Environmental Protection Agency is likely heading to prison after defrauding the federal government out of nearly $1 million."[43] John Beale concocted a scheme to continue drawing a check without doing any of the work.

Question: Why do taxpayers have to spend money for an inauguration party for a president who gets re-elected? Being stuck with the bum for four more years shouldn't warrant more waste and fancy parties. How many homeless people in DC alone could the money have helped? Or disabled vets? But, power freaks aren't concerned about their constituents/voters once they get elected, just themselves.

---

[41] Yahoo! News, Assoc. Press, Pete Yost. Oct. 4, 2012
[42] Yahoo! Autos, Oct. 2012, Justin Hyde
[43] TheFicsalTimes, Dec. 17, 2013, Brianna Ehley

Why is there is a transition of over 2 ½ months after our presidential election, yet the day after the British voted for prime minister, the loser, Mr. Brown moved out of #10 Downing Street and Mr. Cameron moved in. It happened again after the Brexit vote and Cameron left and Ms. May moved in.

All of this waste has contributed to federal government having had annual deficits as much as $1 trillion, so what good are spending cuts (proposed by Congressman Ryan) that amount to $4 trillion over ten years and back-loaded anyway. If it were compared to a typical family budget and they were looking for cuts and savings, it would be as though every Friday the family went out for pizza, paid with a high interest credit card but decided to hold the extra toppings as a way to balance their budget. Staying home and making it themselves would be more effective.

As I said previously, anybody who thinks their taxes or tax rate is to low, the U.S. Treasury accepts donations. Make the check payable to the U.S. Treasury and send a note that it be applied to the debt, it shouldn't end up in the general fund and get wasted.

YOU ARE A FINANCIAL SLAVE. You pay gas taxes, telephone taxes, cigarette taxes, alcohol taxes, luxury taxes, sales taxes, gambling taxes, the embedded taxes of all corporations and the "inflation tax" as Dr. Ron Paul calls it REGARDLESS of whether you pay into the Ponzi scheme or pay income taxes.

CHAPTER EIGHT

ELECTION REFORM

It never ceases to amaze me how a country in which 75% [44] of the population gives lip service to being Christian could find itself governed by dirt-bags, liars and power freaks. Electing people who are not one of the above and are dedicated to solving problems, not just "cashing in" has to be the first step in reforming the election process. Politicians have often tackled "campaign finance reform", however they really need to focus on reforming the entire process which has to include term limits. My suggestion is one 5 year term for the President and Vice-President with a process to have them both recalled after 3 years if the public so wishes. They would be replaced by the Speaker of the House who would not be eligible to seek the next full 5 year term.

The 17th amendment needs to be repealed and senators should again be appointed by the state legislatures and be limited to one 6 year term. Hopefully it will stop carpet baggers (Hilary Clinton) from moving into a state just to run for the Senate. House members would be elected for at most two terms of 3 years. One other reform should be that no family member related by blood or marriage can succeed anyone.

Bill O'Reilly's (FOX News) suggested 18 years for Representatives and Senators. Sorry Bill that's way too long. If we're not going to clean out the swamp at least give more people a chance to "cash in" on the perks of

---

[44]   Topography of Faith, USA Today, Oct. 1, 2012

holding an elected office in Washington. <u>No one</u> needs to hang around for decades. Campaign managers do think you're stupid. Thankfully some lobbyists and public relations firms would go out of business, and the stranglehold of the "incumbency" would be broken. Every elected official would serve without pay or pension. If you aren't interested in true public service, <u>stay home.</u> The President, Vice-President have residences and the Senators and Congressmen have offices better than the homes of many of their constituents. They can sleep and shower at their office and pay for the costs of going home when Congress is not in session out of their own pocket. Why should they live better than the troops they put in harms' way?

The most important reform to the election process is for the League of Women Voters to take back control of the presidential debates and let <u>every constitutionally qualified</u> candidate take part. This nonsense about having to have a certain percent in rigged polls needs to be abandoned. Allow the voters though social media, not some handpicked moderator, to ask the questions. Give every candidate the same question and have a moderator that can say to the candidate, "you didn't answer the question". Are the two major parties afraid of giving the people a real choice? Are they afraid of losing power? Obviously!

The entire presidential election process is way too long. But then what would all the talking heads have to jabber about, surely not something as boring as entitlement reform, tax reform or government waste. There are too many primaries that actually dilute, nullify and render meaningless the vote cast by subsequent states. In 2016 the people spoke and the dirtbags, liars and power freaks that infest both major parties wanted to ignore the voice of the people. Iowa and New Hampshire should never pick the presidential nominee. A National Primary should be held the first weekend in July in all 50 states and the polls should be open on Saturday and Sunday to give every willing American a chance to vote, and yes you will produce a photo ID. Any precinct, city or county that impedes the right to vote of any voter should have all of its ballots disregarded.

Commentators started ballyhooing about the 2016 election and Hillary in January, 2015. Obama is now a lame duck and therefore yesterday's news. It may be time for third party to rise from the ashes of an out of "dead and stinking" Republican Party.

A shorter election cycle would mean the news media will have more time to report on waste, fraud and corruption instead of trying to influence elections that are 2 or 4 years away. Most of the networks will suffer a serious drop in revenue since candidates won't be running as often and Senators won't be elected anymore. MSNBC might even go out of business.

No taxpayer money, from any source, should <u>ever</u> be used to finance any election. A citizen-voter should be allowed to donate any amount they desire as long as they are legally able to cast a ballot for the candidate they are supporting. A candidate could only accept money from those who can cast a ballot in their city, county, state or congressional district. The names of every donation over $1,000 should be listed on an internet site maintained by an independent private agency. Any irregularities before the election should disqualify the candidate and any irregularities found after the election should be grounds for removal from office.

Recently former New York City Mayor Bloomberg committed over $1.7 million of his PAC money to support Clinton crony Terry McAuliffe is his campaign for governor of Virginia even though he can't vote there. While it's not a federal election both of them think Hilary is a mortal lock to be the next president and they probably wanted the Vice President spot, cabinet job or an ambassadorship.

Another example of how morally and ethically bankrupt this practice is, was the 2012 Congressional race in Utah's 4th congressional district. The Democrats were running scared of Mia Love, an African American female who was running as a Republican. She supports the second amendment, smaller government, lower taxes, personal responsibility (as do Libertarians) and might have torn the Black Congressional Caucus apart. (How come there is no White Congressional Caucus? Asian? Latino? Would they be racist?) It seems you can't be an Afro-American and female and be anything but a Democrat/Progressive/Liberal. Obama's Super Pac dumped $100,000 into the campaign to keep her out of Congress.[45] They were successful, but Utah and the country lost. Is that what "life, liberty and the pursuit of happiness" is all about? Fortunately she was elected to Congress in 2014.

Ideally being an attorney should disqualify anyone from holding elected office. They have a conflict of interest in that they should be representing the rights of the people against the power grab of the government. Shakespeare had it right back in the 15th century when he said "If you want to clean up society you must first get rid of all the solicitors (lawyers)" (From Henry VI). For all the lawyers we have in the legislatures we still end up with garbage laws, a totally corrupt legal system not a justice system, zillions of unintended consequences of poorly written laws and politicians who think it's their job is to legislate morality. While it may not be constitutional to disqualify them, voters should never vote for one, especially Hilary.

Though the Republicans were very successful in the 2014 midterm election, they have to learn how to win the PR game. Democrats/liberals/ progressives aren't about substance, they're about perception. But you can't spend perception, and as I outlined they have no record to run on. My ideal candidate for the GOP in the 2016 presidential election would have been a Hispanic female, Christian, articulate, libertarian leaning, Washington outsider, from Texas or Florida, otherwise Hilary wins in a landslide. They were too stupid to find such a person so along came "The Donald" and he shook up the process, and the people spoke.

As I look at what the Republicans have offered up since Ronald Reagan: Bush 41, Dole, Bush 43, McCain and Romney, it's no wonder they lost 4 of the 7 elections. None of them had the charisma or personality of

---

45   Grassroots Action, Sept. 2012, Steve Elliott

Ronald Reagan. The Democrats gave us Mondale, Dukakis, Clinton, Gore, Kerry and Obama. What awful choices.

In my lifetime Jimmy Carter was our most honest president. Ronald Reagan may have been the most effective president. In 2016 the voters should have taken a longer look at Rand Paul, Ben Carson, and Mike Huckabee if they aren't going to nominate a woman. All three are devote Christians, honest, family men, and understand government's many failings.

My Prediction was that Hilary didn't have to campaign, waste/spend money, or conduct an internet campaign. She can wait until Labor Day of 2016 and any Democrat that thinks he/she can beat her is dreaming. I admired Bernie Sanders for running, but in the end he accomplished nothing thanks to the rigged delegate (super-delegates) process. She was ahead 500 – 0 before the first votes were cast. Hello more and more socialism if she'd have won. Thankfully the "silent majority" didn't stay silent and Donald Trump won.

CHAPTER NINE

SOLUTIONS

Over the course of my lifetime I believe the government was involved in cover-ups of the assassinations John Kennedy (1963), Robert Kennedy (1968), and Martin Luther King (1968). I believe the Department of (In) Justice also covered up the loss of life at Ruby Ridge (ID), Waco (TX), Oklahoma City and on flight 800. The "coup de grace" was 911. While I may not consider myself a "conspiracy theorist" I know from experience the government lies constantly. They justify it by claiming "national security" or "need to know". Since 9/11 everything is now a matter of national security or some state of emergency.

Before Americans can begin to fix a government that is totally broken and has made financial slaves of everyone we have to *STOP THE LIES* and come to grips with the idea that the solutions have to be AMERICAN solutions based on ethics and morality, not Democrat or Republican, white or non-white, citizens or illegals, rich or poor, gay or straight, or any other special interest. First and foremost we must act as "One nation under God", then as Americans and a distant third the member of some political group.

Gay rights, abortion, gun control, immigration, global warming and human trafficking may all be issues the country faces but they do not affect us as much as radical Islamic Terrorists, worthless money, waste at all levels of government, courts that don't respect the constitution, abuse of power, an education system that doesn't educate, a phony war on drugs, undeclared wars and a general moral decay in our society.

The size of ALLLLLLLLLLLLLLLLL government has to be reduced. Washington spits on the Tenth Amendment on a daily basis. Too many of the dirt-bags, liars and power freaks in Washington came out of state government and seem to forget what the federal government tried to force upon them and how they use to wail against Washington regulations. In order to "clean out the swamp", the voters have to demand a new Grand Bargain with the America people that includes ALL of the following:

1) <u>Put GOD back in to our lives.</u> God does not make a mistake. HE expects we share our good fortune with those in need, allow school prayer, ban abortion on demand, stop rewarding laziness, realize pornography is not free speech, marriage is between a man and a woman and we're all called to spread HIS message.

Roy Moore, Chief Justice of the Alabama Supreme Court who was removed from office for not taking down the Ten Commandments from his courtroom foyer, and later re-elected, wrote the following poem:

America the beautiful. Or so it used to be.
Land of the Pilgrims' pride; I'm glad they'll never see.
Babies piled in dumpsters, Abortion on demand,
Oh, sweet land of liberty; your house is on the sand.
Our children wander aimless poisoned by cocaine
Choosing to indulge their lusts, when God has said abstain
From sea to shining sea our nation turns away
From the teaching of God's love and a need to always pray.
We've kept God in our temple how callous we have grown.
When earth is but his footstool, and Heaven is His throne.
We've voted in a government that's rotting at the core,
Appointing Godless Judges; who throw reason out the door.
Too soft to place a killer in a well-deserved tomb,
But brave enough to kill a baby before he leaves the womb.

You think that God's not angry, that out land's a moral slum?
How much longer will He wait before His judgment comes?
How are we to face our God from whom we cannot hide?
What then is left for us to do, but stem this evil tide?
If we who are His children, will humbly turn and pray;
Seek His holy face and mend our evil way:
Then God will hear from heaven and forgive our sins,
He'll heal our sickly land and those who live within,
But America the beautiful, if you don't -- then you will see
A sad but Holy God withdraw His hand from Thee.

2) <u>Pass a balance budget amendment and a line item veto.</u> Any solution must address the fiscal irresponsibility in Washington. That solution has to start with really balancing the budget. A balanced budget means choices, which may mean layoffs, reduction of giveaways, shuttering agencies, reducing government pensions, establish real competitive bidding and an overall reduction in the size of government. No pay for sitting members of Congress and staff or pensions for ANY ex-president, vice-president, congressperson, congressional staff, senator, federal judge, and armed service members above the rank of major until the budget is balanced. Stealing from the social security system is not balancing the budget. A balanced budget amendment and a real debt ceiling would begin to encourage investment and put some value in those "federal reserve notes" you may have in your pocket.

3) <u>Abolish the IRS and adopt a national retail sales tax.</u> The rate to be constantly monitored as the true cost of running the government is investigated. In 1913 we had a "flat tax" (the first $50,000 of income was taxed at 1%. That covered 90% of the population). In 1982 Congress came close to a "flat tax" when they reduced the tax brackets to just two. We've been there and done that, not interested.

4) <u>Abolish the Federal Reserve</u>. Former Congressman Jim Traficant also wrote: "The Federal Reserve System will be audited" but raised the question "Do you really believe that a true audit will be conducted"? I predict that any audit, regardless of the entity charged with the responsibility to do that work, will be nothing more than an official certification proclaiming the greatness of the Fed. When it's over, it will make the Warren Commission (JFK Assassination) and 911 Commission reports seem like the minutes of a school board meeting." Three outstanding books on the Federal Reserve, and why it must be abolished, are *Creature from Jekyll Island* by G. Edward Griffin, *High Priests of Treason* by Mel Stamper and *End the Fed* by Dr. Ron Paul.

5) <u>Repeal the Patriot Act and stop spying on us;</u> Shahid Buttar, the executive director of the Bill of Rights Defense Committee, had an article that appeared in the *Youngstown Vindicator*, October 25, 2011 said "The Justice Department's own internal watchdog has documented numerous abuses of Patriot Act powers. The federal government has issued thousands of improper National Security Letters. The Patriot Act has also been used by the Departments of Justice and Treasury to seize charities without due process, even though the work of such organizations could advance U.S. interests by alleviating suffering in war-torn area and winning hearts and minds. The same provisions have enabled investigations of peace, labor and immigrant rights activists in Chicago, Minneapolis and Los Angeles for what essentially amount to thought crimes.

But the abuses extend well beyond the Patriot Act, constructing a whole even worse than the sum of its parts. Under Bush—and with the later support of the Obama administration----the National Security Agency launched a secret dragnet warrantless wiretapping scheme, which became public only because intrepid journalists (and Edward Snowden) risked prosecution to reveal it. What a country!!!! Even though every federal court that ever reviewed the program on its merits declared it unconstitutional, Congress authorized the agency's wire-tapping through legislation in 2008 and immunized telecommunications companies that participated in it.

Under Bush, the attorney general's guidelines governing FBI operations were overhauled, allowing investigative tactics from the infamous COINTELPRO era, such as infiltrating constitutionally protected ideological groups----on the basis of a secret legal standard that has never been disclosed. And even though the CIA is prohibited from operating within the United States, it has smeared critics and trained law enforcement in counterproductive profiling techniques." NEVER has our government been less accountable to We the People.

6) <u>Make social security contributions voluntary</u>. Once Social Security is voluntary America will find out real fast how solvent it is not; it's the second largest component of the federal budget. There is no reforming it by politicians.

7) <u>Get out of foreign entanglements, protect our own borders</u>, build a wall, clean up our streets and stop occupying other countries. Let the United Nations be the "policeman of the world". Bring our troops home. War is, and has always been, about pillage, plunder and PROFIT. We have created a monster. President Eisenhower warned America to beware of the military industrial complex. (i.e. defense contractors)

8) <u>Shut down</u> HUD, FNMA, Sallie Mae, FHA, Departments of Energy, Education, Agriculture, Interior, Transportation, Commerce and Labor, stop subsidizing the post office and reduce the prison population. Let the states develop policies and programs for education, health care, agriculture, housing, roads and energy development. If any of those agencies are performing some indispensable function let the states hire any displaced workers. Homeland Security and FEMA have to be totally revamped as well. Americans should be asking why politicians

are not cutting their taxes or eliminating their taxes. With all our debt, and social programs we don't have streets paved with gold, the healthiest population, the most educated population, the safest streets, the safest bridges, no one hungry or homeless and medical care for all. But they're keeping us same from terrorists!

Education MUST be a parental or local matter. With all the money the feds have thrown away our graduation rates and intelligence levels are going down. The media glamorizes singers, dancers, athletes rather than ministers, teachers, parents, caregivers, entrepreneurs and laborers. How many of those celebrities/athletes are now broke, homeless, unemployed, divorced or dead-beat dads? According to Sports Illustrated sixty percent of professional athletes in the NFL or NBA will fall into one of those categories within 2-5 years of being away from the sport.

9) <u>Restore and Respect States Rights</u>. The federal government has only have two legitimate Functions #1 PROTECT our constitutional rights (not steal them), and #2 protect our borders. (9-11 and Hurricane Katrina proved how inept they were that). Every other function of government can be done and should be handled and funded at the city, county, state level.

10) <u>Enact Term Limits</u>. One 5 year term for the president, two 3 year terms for House members and one 6 year terms for Senators who are appointed by, and can be removed by the state legislatures. What Federal judges are left, after we stop making everything a "federal" crime, would be limited to one 10 year term subject to recall of the people. They will pay into the giant Ponzi scheme (for as long as it exists) and receive no bonuses or special pension benefit. There will be a mandatory age. (my vote 75) The country would save billions and not have to be inundated with name-calling ads. Hopefully some newspapers and networks will go

broke. The money spent buying political favors could be spent on real help, from private donors, for the less fortunate.

In the final analysis none of these ideas are going to come about unless you the voter realizes it's long past time to send all the dirt-bags, liars and power freaks packing. Drain the swamp. *Stop Repeat Offenders, RE-ELECT NOBODY* should be a bumper sticker on every car in this country. The fact that they won't go away voluntarily proves my point. Politicians claim you have the power to "limit their term" at the ballot box, but when the choice offered is the lesser of two evils the voters seem to check their memory at the door of the polling place.

My challenge to all of you who claim to Independent, Libertarian, Tea Party, Green Party, Reform Party, Beach Party, Beer Party or any other third party, is go to the polls in 2018 and vote against the incumbents, even if you have never voted or don't know anything about the candidates. (Nevada is trying to promote "none of the above". Here's hoping.) I don't care who he/she is or which party they are from. You are the balance of power in this country and with that power can send a loud and clear message to politicians everywhere. You won't show up in any of the rigged polls. All the "factually inaccurate" campaign statements will be meaningless. All the campaign money wasted. All the negative ads in vain. The talking heads, pollsters and strategists will have even more egg on their face. By 2020 if the rest of Washington isn't either kissing your backside or heading for the hills, send them packing too.

CHAPTER TEN

HOW HILARY LOST A
RIGGED ELECTION

The Democratic nominating process was stacked against any challengers to Hilary right from the start. The party elite gave her a 500+ to 0 lead before the first person went to the polls in any primary. They called them "super delegates". They were in fact D's who wanted favors, jobs and appointments from Hilary once she was elected. I admire Bernie Sanders for waging a campaign, though futile against her. He would have done better. The Dem elites began to believe their own rigged polls that she was going to win.

While visiting family in Ohio in the summer of '16 my wife and I took in a standup comedy show at a Hollywood Casino. During his act one of the comics took a poll of the audience (of about 100) regarding the election. Of those that voiced an opinion it was overwhelming for Trump. He made the point that he performed all over the country, asked the same questions and got the same results. He said "don't believe the polls". I never did. Trump carried the heavily Democratic county where I grew up, and won Ohio easily. That county also went for Reagan in '80 and '84, yet voted overwhelmingly for Jim Traficant, a Dem, for their Congressional representative. The Dem strategists just don't get it. To quote one of their own, "It's the economy stupid", not gay rights, abortion rights, equal pay, and gun control. The voters aren't quite as stupid as the D's and the media think.

Mr. Nixon's famous "silent majority" was/is totally disgusted with Washington, and rates politicians lower than used car salesmen. Yet, strategists don't give a damn. The D's thought blacks, gays, trial lawyers, union members, Jewish voters, and women would flock to their anointed one. All you had to do was go to a Trump rally and see the size of his crowds to know she was in trouble, and he didn't have to pay his supporters to show up. This country made a major mistake by not voting for a businessman, Ross Perot, in 1992, but got it right in 2016.

Hilary was treated as if she was above the law over Benghazi, her personal server, and the phony foundation. ANYBODY else would have been indicted. The government stole 8 ½ years of my life, and the lives of over 1,000 others I spent time with, over chicken shit nonsense compared to her. It seems that if your name is Clinton you get a free pass on anything. I want to puke when I hear that we "are a nation of laws" or that the "rule of law must be upheld".........If she's not indicted they should release every federal prisoner who is a non-violent, first time offender.

For the record, she did not win the popular vote. Fifty-two percent of the voters voted for someone else. She may have gotten the most votes but that statistics mean NOTHING. The Electoral College is the only count that matters. Even with leaked debate questions, a billion dollar name calling contest, lack of any real achievements, out spending Trump and an absolute media bias she lost a rigged election. All her "experts", "strategists", "gurus" didn't understand the fact that the country wanted a non-politician, not a Bush or Clinton. Trump was the only candidate the R's could have nominated would could beat her and she underestimated him. I'd call that poetic justice.

THE ELECTORAL COLLEGE

The eleven most populated states can elect a person POTUS even if they are not on the ballot in the other 39 states, and yes the candidate could have lost the popular vote. The very reason the founders set up the EC is wrought with fallacies. Your vote really doesn't count in small states, unless you're the last state to close its polls or every state has been close and they're still counting a particular small western state.

Here are those votes:

California 55
Texas 38
New York 29
Florida 29
Illinois 20
Pennsylvania 20
Ohio 18
Georgia 16
Michigan 16
North Carolina 15
New Jersey 14

Total 270

Rest assured, the political strategists know it, which is one reason they want to keep third parties out of the process, because the EC does not require the "winner" to have 50.1% of the states' votes to get all the electoral votes. (Nebraska and Maine do split their electoral votes, though they have only a handful of votes). "Slick Willie" is living proof of that since 57% of the people voted AGAINST him in '92 and 51% again in '96.

What keeps the rest of the states in play is that too many voters California and New York would vote for Miss Piggy/Kermit the Frog as long as they had a "D" behind their name. Texas, Florida, Georgia tend to counterbalance that idiocy. Ohio, Pennsylvania and Michigan tend to go back and forth. Illinois leans Democratic largely because of Chicago. North Carolina is more conservative and New Jersey needs work. "Bridge-gate" didn't help conservatives in New Jersey.

I believe a strong Libertarian/3rd party candidate who is liberal on social issues and strong on monetary issues could win all of these states in a three way race. If 2016 proved anything it's that the public is fed up with both the "D's" and the "R's". I saw a statistic that said 97 million registered voters, didn't vote, though America has never had a presidential election in which 90% plus voted. Sixty percent seems to be the high water mark. Though I believe they did in fact vote, by not showing up they said NONE OF THE ABOVE, and rather loudly. Ninety-seven million is more votes than either Hilary or Trump got.

Hilary knew she had California, New York and Illinois in her back pocket which accounted for 38% of the 270 EC votes that she need to win. She sure wasn't criticizing the process or questioning the vote then. If she split the rest of the country she was a shoo-in, but the undecided and the never voted all went for Trump and saved the country.

Good Luck trying to abolish it. You are never going to get 38 states to ratify a constitutional amendment, because in that process all states have just one vote which does mean something.

If you sometimes think your vote doesn't count, pray the country never goes to a popular vote scenario, those 11 states will dictate the election. People in Alaska and Wyoming could stay home. The D's are whining about Hilary winning the popular vote, yet if you exclude California and the illegal votes, Trump won the popular vote. Should any one large populated state be the deciding factor????

Now the D's are afraid they may be on the outside looking in for at least the next 8 years, and hopefully longer if the R's or the Libertarians find the right woman by 2024. But even worse the Dems are already worried about losing Senate seats in the '18 mid-term elections.

EPILOG

A book like this is never ending because of all the abusive, incompetent agencies and bureaucrats that infest Washington D.C. I started writing this one in the summer of 2010 while a guest of the government, and forced myself to stop in early 2014. Yet everyday there is a new lie/fake news involving abuse of authority, government waste, fraud, the need for prison reform, tax reform, the rich don't pay enough, corporate greed, gay rights, the war on terrorism and everything that comes out of the mouth of a politician. The Presidential primary election season of 2015-2016 was the proverbial "icing on the cake". The "establishment" (whatever that is) decided they couldn't care less what the citizen voters wanted and did everything they could to derail Trump and Sanders. Never have I seen the "will of the people" so wantonly disregarded. Remember they think you're stupid.

Here's a short list of events that happened in 2013-2015 that validate my premise:

Thad Cochran (R) had to recruit Democratic voters (2014) to hold his Senate seat in Mississippi's primary. It's as though his attitude was "if I can't have it, neither can the Tea Party." I hoped the Tea Partiers would have thrown him out.

The VA Scandal, and nobody goes to jail. They never did anything for my dad. I tried to get Aid & Assistance for him from the VA in the May of 2012, on the advice of one of their representatives, of less than

$2,000. He died in September, 2012 and my mother is still waiting for a response from the VA.

Bank of America, that "to big fail" bank, the government owned and forced to absorb Merrill Lynch, among others, is hit with $17 billion settlement involving mortgages. Whose money do you think really is paying this debt since the government owns and controls them?

Lois Lerner, the central figure in the IRS targeting of Tea Party organizations, ignores a Congressional subpoena. It seems the subpoena lacks any teeth. Mysteriously somebody found her lost e-mails. She just waited out the clock and retired, and she allegedly gave information to the DOJ with authorization. In 2016 Hilary also ignores a Congressional subpoena. If they don't have teeth, why issue them.

The Hobby Lobby Case that is a clear intrusion into small business and a wanton disrespect for religious views.

IRAQ mess comes back to haunt us.

Politicians are rejoicing the deficit is only $500,000,000,000, which means the government still borrow fifteen cents of every dollar spent, on top the $19+ billion in debt America has piled up.

Overseas accounts, tax havens, inversions and mergers all designed to circumvent/avoid the corporate income tax and are PERFECTLY LEGAL. A very good reason to abolish the income tax, though Mr. Trump is hoping to bring that money back to this country.

Immigration: the selective enforcement of the laws has now led to thousands of children flooding our country and taxing our health system, education system and the entire immigration process.

Some nonsense about a "war on women" because we don't give out free control pills, condone abortion or give them the same pay. Should we be giving out free condoms? Be performing free vasectomies? Who put a gun to your head to take a job that didn't pay what you think you're worth? Hasn't Obama created millions of jobs???? What?? They don't pay enough!!!!

Lots of government propaganda about waiting to collect YOUR social security benefits as though collecting them early is not "patriotic".

The Edward Snowden revelations about government spying. Wow, the government spies on us!!!!!!!

"Obama-phone" Program Filled with Abuse.

Proposing to raise the Federal Highway gas tax hurts the poor......idiots.

Jonathan Gruber openly stating what the Democratic strategists/pollsters believe, Americans are stupid.

Ferguson, Mo. shooting and violence. Where was the LOCAL clergy and religious leaders?

DOJ, IRS secretly probing Koch Brothers for Democrats. (They give money to conservative causes)

FAKE NEWS has crept into the internet life. The Huffington Post ran an unsubstantiated internet story that the cost of a military jet could house every homeless person in the U.S. with $600,000 home. The cost of the program was allegedly $400 billion, which equates to 660,000 $600,000 homes. The story was ludicrous because the ENTIRE military budget is about $600 Billion.

Social Security's $300 million computer system, six years in the making still doesn't work. Congress to block promoting the acting director.

A Republican Congressman and former FBI agent pleads guilty to tax charges.

IRS deliberately withheld its investigation into conservative targeting until after the 2012 elections.

Ted Cruz sabotages Ben Carson in Iowa……..

Dingell family (father, son and son's wife) has held either the 15th (later the12th) Michigan Congressional seat since 1933. What??? Nobody else in Michigan is qualified to be a Congresscritter?

Ruby Ridge, Sarah Weaver's book; total dirtbags - changed "rules of engagement"—the federal government paid $3.1M in damages, and nobody went to jail except Randy Weaver. There is an alphabet soup list of domestic terrorist organizations.

Since the mid-term elections of 2010 I thought America was waking up, but 2016 was critical mass as to whether they truly have. GO TRUMP!!!!

Printed in the United States
By Bookmasters